# THIN PATHS

Julia Blackburn has written five books of non-fiction – *Charles Waterton*, *The Emperor's Last Island*, *Daisy Bates in the Desert*, *Old Man Goya* and *With Billie* – a family memoir, *The Three of Us*, which won the 2009 J. R. Ackerley Award, and two novels, *The Book of Colour* and *The Leper's Companions*, both of which were shortlisted for the Orange Prize. She is the author of seventeen short stories specially commissioned by BBC Radio, a selection of which were published in *My Animals and Other Family*, and four radio plays, including *The Spellbound Horses* which was broadcast in 2011.

D1100812

JULIA BLACKBURN

# Thin Paths

Journeys In and Around an Italian
Mountain Village

**VINTAGE BOOKS**
London

Published by Vintage 2012

2 4 6 8 10 9 7 5 3 1

First published in Great Britain in 2011 by
Jonathan Cape

Vintage
Random House, 20 Vauxhall Bridge Road,
London SW1V 2SA

www.vintage-books.co.uk

Addresses for companies within The Random House Group Limited
can be found at: www.randomhouse.co.uk/offices.htm

The Random House Group Limited Reg. No. 954009

A CIP catalogue record for this book
is available from the British Library

ISBN 9780099549420

The Random House Group Limited supports The Forest Stewardship
Council (FSC®), the leading international forest certification
organisation. Our books carrying the FSC label are printed on FSC®
certified paper. FSC is the only forest certification scheme endorsed
by the leading environmental organisations, including Greenpeace.
Our paper procurement policy can be found at
www.randomhouse.co.uk/environment

Typeset by Palimpsest Book Production Limited,
Falkirk, Stirlingshire

Printed and bound by CPI Group (UK) Ltd, Croydon, CR0 4YY

# PEOPLE IN THE STORY

Adriana 1935–

Agostina 1932–

Armando 1925–

Arturo (Adriana's husband, son of Old Tunin and la Muta) 1927–2004

Batti (who was born in our house) 1938–2009

Clelia (the bonesetter) 1925–2010

Eliana (Adriana's daughter) 1968–

Giovanin (the shepherd) 1935–

Ida (Armando's sister–in–law and wife of Pino) 1929–

La Muta (wife of Old Tunin) 1890–1983

Nanda (Adriana's sister and owner of the shop) 1932–

Nella (the retired postmistress) 1948–

Pino (Ida's husband, Armando's brother) 1922–2004

Rinuccia (Adriana's neighbour) 1927–2009

Terzina (Young Tunin's wife) 1927–

Tunin da Muta (Old Tunin) 1898–1992

Tunin (Young Tunin or Tuninetto, son of Old Tunin,
husband of Terzina) 1923–

# CONTENTS

ix

It's as if time past, time present and time future is stretched out around us like a vast landscape and we are walking through it on a tracery of thin paths.

PART ONE

BEING HERE

# A Little Kingdom

Herman first came here by mistake. It was in May 1994 and he was walking the Alta Via, the high path, which follows the backbone of the mountains above the Italian Riviera town of Ventimiglia, close to the French border, as far as La Spezia and the Bay of Lerici, where Shelley's body was washed ashore so casually on the pale sand.

To walk the length of the path takes about a month. There are refuges along the way where you can get food and shelter, but there are also long stretches where you can walk for a couple of days without seeing any human habitation.

He had been doing this kind of walking all his life. Sometimes I would get a postcard: he was with friends crossing the Sinai Desert on camel and on foot, and they had just reached the Monastery of Saint Catherine where suddenly they were confronted by busloads of tourists and how strange that was after so much silence. He was in the Abruzzi region, not all that far from Rome and one night he was woken by a deep growling and roaring sound, which he thought might be a bear, but he learnt later that it was only the mating call of a red deer.

In the year that his daughter was born he wrote to say he was just home after three weeks in the mountains of Corsica, sleeping out all the time, and he'd seen no one apart from a group of French Legionnaires who were lying like babies on their backs in a meadow of flowers, sucking at tubes of sweetened condensed milk to give them energy before they continued with their training.

In one letter he explained he had found the secret of travelling light: he didn't carry a tent, only a sleeping bag and a groundsheet, and along with a couple of litres of water, he took dried muesli, dried milk powder, teabags and bouillon cubes, and that was enough. I used to try to imagine what such a journey was like, plodding along step by step from dawn until dusk, looking back to see where you have come from, looking forward towards where you are going and how the mind must grow quiet while the body is so busy.

Anyway, there he was on the Alta Via and he had been walking for a few days and had almost reached the highest pass, when the way was blocked by great banks of snow and he had to go down into the valley below. He followed the remains of an elegant mule track which led to a stone chapel, built with such softly rounded edges that it looked as if it had been moulded in clay. The chapel stood on a grassy mound that undulated on all sides like a tiny range of hills. Above the locked blue-painted door was written *Santuario di San Antonio* and the date in Roman numerals: 1793.

The mule track continued to descend through a forest of chestnut trees, the carcasses of old trunks hemmed in by thickets of young saplings. There was a humpbacked bridge over a stream and then he was entering a village. The houses were for the most part in good order, but their doors were firmly bolted and the shutters over the windows were closed. The village was perched on the top of a perpendicular cliff, with overgrown vegetable gardens laid out like little carpets to the very edge of the drop. He passed a walled cemetery and was walking along a narrow asphalted road when a woman in a battered Renault 4 stopped and offered him a lift.

She was very friendly and she spoke French as well as Italian. She said the village was her childhood home and she came whenever she could, just to look around. 'This was the village of the shepherds,' she said. 'It once had seven hundred inhabitants but now there are only two old men who are here for most of the year. In summer we took the sheep and goats to the high pastures and when winter was approaching we brought them down to the coast. We were used to going everywhere on foot. There was no road to the end of the valley until the 1970s.'

They drove along one side of a gorge, the steep curtains of rock as smooth as dripping candle wax and coloured in unlikely yellows and oranges. They passed a couple of tiny villages and the woman dropped him off at a hotel

in a town that looked like a fortress, the houses arched over the cobbled streets, making a honeycomb of tunnels.

He stayed there for a couple of nights and then set off back to the Alta Via, avoiding the snow at the head of the valley. When he reached the crest of the mountains he had a view all the way down through the steeply interconnecting folds of land as far as the shimmering triangle of the Mediterranean Sea. The little kingdom stayed in his mind.

# Him and Me

Herman and I had been living our separate lives for almost a generation. We first met in 1966 when I was eighteen and he was twenty-nine. Then five years later we parted for good as they say, after a lot of muddle and drama. He was in Holland and I was in England and we kept in contact, but only vaguely, and on the rare occasions when we met it was with other people standing around, conversations fluttering and jumping on all sides.

Then in 1995 he sent me a postcard: a painting of an old tumbled-down cottage with smoke billowing from the chimney and a smiling woman in the garden. 'I've just bought a ruin in the mountains of Liguria,' he wrote. 'You'd like it here. It's a mixture of North Wales and the west coast of Majorca.'

'That sounds nice,' I replied and in my mind's eye I created an imaginary landscape in which grey Presbyterian chapels and wet sheep in a cold wind rubbed shoulders with Catholic shrines and lizards sunbathing on limestone rocks under a blue sky. I put the postcard in a photograph album without pausing to wonder why.

In the autumn of 1998 another postcard arrived. It showed a very odd, brightly coloured painting from a church in a place I'd never heard of. He said he'd just come back from a walk over the border into France – that

was where he'd got the card – and his ruin was now a house, two little houses in fact, with enough room for guests as long as they didn't mind shiny black scorpions and hairy centipedes and hardly a scrap of flat ground to stand on. I thanked him for the card and said how much I liked the image, and put it in the album alongside the first one.

And then we spoke on the phone and in February 1999 we had a brief meeting, and all the time the talk between us went so fast and there was so much more to say that he laughed and asked if I would like to come and visit him in the mountains. So I bought a pair of climbing boots and on the morning of 5 April he met me at Nice airport, and his little dog danced a welcome as if she and I were also old friends.

He'd changed, of course; grey curls instead of black, a bald bit on the top of his head and deeper lines cut into his face, but I kept seeing the young man and the old man superimposed in the one image and we seemed to continue where we had left off and as if we had never been apart.

It was already dark when we crossed the border from France into Italy, so I saw hardly anything as the car began its laborious climb up the valley. After a while we went past a line of houses illuminated by a few streetlamps, then we turned abruptly to the right next to a war memorial and, after counting nine hairpin bends, we were following a narrow dirt track, the branches of olive trees brushing against the car. We stopped and with the help of a torch I could see the silhouette of two small houses side by side on a steep slope and all on their own in the middle of a black nowhere.

The following morning we were enveloped in a thick white cloud, which confirmed the North Wales aspect of my imagined landscape, but when the cloud lifted everything was much more wild than I had thought possible. Immediately opposite but with a little side valley in between, was the flank of a mountain with a thin covering of trees and precipitous rock faces leading to a bare ridge dusted with the remains of the winter snow, and when I turned to look inland a mass of other mountains were jostling shoulder to shoulder into the far distance like a tumultuous ocean. But in spite of such looming presences there was no feeling of being trapped, because when you stood on the little terrace your eye could race down the entire length of the valley until it reached the sea.

8

Every day of the four days of that visit, we put on walking boots and went striding off in one direction or another. We followed the path through the oak woods immediately behind the house, stopping at the walled cemetery to look at the portraits on the marble tombs of the people who were buried there. There were several young men who had died in the final months of the last world war and several very old men and women who were well into their ninetieth decade when they finally let go of life. One smiling man was shown standing next to his donkey as if the two of them had gone into the ground together.

We reached the square of the upper village where two churches faced each other like rivals. The newer one was freshly painted and looked like an iced wedding cake while the older, smaller and much prettier building had a dangerous crack in its wall stuffed rather haphazardly with blue tarpaulin and on its clock face the time was always ten to one.

Now the path passed a stone basin for washing clothes; a toad emerged from among the maidenhair ferns and struggled to lift its awkward body up the side of a wall, but it kept falling back. There were baby salamanders in the water and when I put my face close to the surface I could see them suspended in stillness, the little ruffs of gills beneath their heads making them look as elegant as courtiers from another age.

The way was marked by shrines: here was a wooden Virgin spreading her cloak to give shelter to a kneeling man with a pointy black beard, and here was an angel reaching down to the sinners in hell. The flames that surrounded them looked as soft and welcoming as a field of wheat. Most of the shrines contained a jam jar or a vase filled with a little bunch of flowers and even when the flowers were long since dead, it gave the sense of people walking this way and pausing for a moment.

It began to rain and the little dog refused to go any further, so after a while we turned round and went back the way we had come. My hair had gone all curly in the rain and he remembered how I used to be so desperate to keep it straight, flattening it, pinning it down and even ironing it under a sheet of brown paper. I once refused to go with him to a Janis Joplin concert because I couldn't face the outside world with a curly fringe.

For one of our walks we planned to skirt around the flank of the mountain. The line of the path was easy to see from our terrace and it began very auspiciously, pottering along with confidence and clarity, but then suddenly it dived into a tangle of raspberry canes and hazelnut bushes and disappeared. We tried to retrace our steps but couldn't decide where it was that we had been, so we blundered on, working our way down the slope until we had entered a forest of larch and oak and chestnut.

We reached what seemed like a path, but maybe it had only been made by the sharp feet of the wild pigs, because it vanished as abruptly as it had appeared. We crossed the dry bed of a stream cluttered with the broken trunks of trees. We clambered precariously over a landslide of rock and fresh earth, and by now we were utterly lost, struggling forward and turning back again, even though we could see the two houses watching us implacably from the other side of the valley.

It was growing dark and we thought we might have to make ourselves a nest, where we could sleep like the children in the fairy tale, lying among the dried leaves and the roots of trees, but then we came across an empty beer can and a wooden gate standing all on its own with nothing to keep out or to let in and that gave us a sense of getting somewhere. Close to the gate was a black water pipe, lolling on the ground like a great snake. We followed the meanderings of the pipe and it eventually led us to a narrow cement road that hairpinned down to the road and the lower village.

The shop was open, its neon sign beaming a welcome. A bell chimed as we entered and the woman called Nanda appeared from among the cheeses

and saucepans, the votive candles and firelighters, the artichokes and sacks of dried chestnuts. I hadn't many words of Italian, but it was easy to understand that Nanda was full of concern and felt it was far too late for us to be walking all the way home again.

She went out into the street and shouted towards the balcony above the butcher's shop; the butcher appeared like a character in a Restoration comedy, dressed in his flapping pyjamas. As he had clearly just woken from a deep sleep, Nanda went to the house of the post office lady, who was still up, and she fetched her car and bundled us into it and drove us home. We had dried cod stew for supper, which we had been told would be delicious if boiled in white wine with a bay leaf and some garlic, although it tasted every bit as odd and leathery as it looked.

# Learning to Speak

The future we were heading towards began to take shape: a thin path vanishing into the distance. Day by day, step by step. Stones placed against trees where you could sit and stare. Unexpected turnings that might take you into an unfamiliar landscape.

During the first year, when we were still busy organising our changed lives, we were often apart, so we sent each other faxes, which spewed like ectoplasm from the fax machine, the thin curling paper covered with drawings and words. 'One thing that is very important to me is having the drawers of a cupboard kept closed,' I wrote and I made a drawing of a prim, house-proud lady with her arms folded; it was only later that I noticed how rarely I closed drawers: everywhere the legs of tights and the arms of T-shirts were struggling to escape from captivity.

'Order is important for me as well,' he said gravely, and he sent me a drawing of the strange chaos of his studio, where mysterious objects had drifted into heaps as if carried there by the surge of a high tide.

'From now on we will always be together. Even when we are apart we will be together,' he wrote and with that I was briefly afraid of the fact of death, when one of us might have to go ahead while the other stayed behind.

We came to the valley as often as possible. I got used to the scorpions who held themselves very still when they felt cornered, so it was easy to catch them in a glass and watch them turning in slow and defensive circles, curled tail at the ready, before throwing them into the garden. I could identify the floating silhouettes of eagles and peregrine falcons, and the ravens who always announced themselves with hoarse cries as they trundled through the sky. I became less startled by the harshness of the mountain soil crammed with so many stones that you can only dig into it with a sharp hacking implement called a *zappa*. People here like to say that if you are born with a *zappa* in your hands you will go on working with the *zappa* for the rest of your life.

I had never learnt Italian and had only a few phrases floating vaguely in my head, and nothing else to be going along with apart from hopeful gestures and guesswork using bits of French and Spanish. I noticed that nobody seemed to mind my haphazardness, particularly the old people who were used to speaking in the local dialect, so for them Italian was also a foreign language that never sounded quite right. I smiled and nodded and they smiled and nodded back, and sometimes I tried to speak and they had no idea what I was attempting to say, or they spoke in a flurry of words to which I had no answer. But we were pleased to be communicating and that was the point.

Nanda, the owner of the village shop, and Eliana, her niece, became my language teachers. They always spoke slowly and clearly, watching my face to make sure I understood their words and listening very carefully to my attempts at an answer. They explained that they had learnt this way of talking because of Eliana's grandmother, who was deaf and dumb and was known as La Muta, the Silent One. She could lip-read, but more importantly she seemed to know what people were saying to her just by staring at the expressions on their faces.

So I would come into the shop and point to something among the jumble of items for sale and one of the two ladies would give me its name and wait for me to repeat it, correcting my shy pronunciation. And if I brought a stumbling shopping list, they would offer me what I seemed to be requesting, holding up a hairbrush or a packet of butter, a votive candle or a jar of honey.

I began to prepare whole sentences before I walked in through the narrow door and they would patiently disentangle the sense from the nonsense and steer me through. One day I proudly recited my own translation of a little poem:

> The rain it raineth every day
> Upon the just and unjust fella
> But more upon the just because
> The unjust's got the just's umbrella

> *La pioggia piove ogni giorno*
> *Sopra il giusto e l'ingiusto uomo*
> *Pero piu sopra il uomo giusto*
> *Perche il uomo ingiusto ha robato l'ombrello del uomo giusto*

Nanda was on her own that afternoon. She listened with her head on one side like a bird and when I had finished she didn't laugh, but said it was quite true, the unjust have always cheated and stolen and nothing changes. Then by way of thanks she rummaged about under the counter and produced a book of fairy tales, which she gave me as a present.

The next time I came I told the two of them that once a long time ago there lived a fisherman who was so unlucky he didn't even manage to catch an anchovy to bring home to his wife and his son, and with that they applauded from behind the counter, raising their hands like an audience in an auditorium.

———————————•———————————

One day I met Agostina. She was in her garden and I suppose it must have been the early summer because she had a cotton headscarf tied tightly across her forehead, and the simple uniform of a cotton dress, coming just to the knees, and an apron with a big front pocket for carrying things. Ankle socks and strong shoes.

Agostina was picking flowers and she looked up and greeted me. She was in her seventies, small but very straight-bodied as many of the women are from carrying heavy loads on their heads. Her face was lean and well-sculpted, with heavily lidded blue eyes and a sharp nose.

She told me she was picking flowers for her son's grave, but I am not sure how I understood this. Was it just that I took the words *mio figlio* and then added the word *morto* and looked at the flowers in her hands and the tears streaming down her face?

'Three years ago,' she said, holding up three fingers to show me how recent it was, 'and he was young, only forty-two,' again using the fingers of her hand.

'You have the flowers,' she said, presenting me with them. 'There are many more in my garden,' and she made a little gesture towards them growing all around her: the lilies and the agapanthus, the dahlias and the pots of geraniums.

So I took the flowers and thanked her, and she held my hand in both of hers for a moment and looked into my eyes, the tears following the lines in her cheeks. Then she smiled and the conversation was over.

Later, when I understood more Italian, Agostina and her husband some-times stopped close to our house on their way to their olive trees, or I saw her in the upper village and she would invite me to drink a glass of wine with her. That was how I began to pick up little snippets of stories about the people here and the lives they had known.

Sitting at the metal-topped table in her kitchen, Agostina told me how her father had died. This was in 1970, she said, but it felt like yesterday. It was a Sunday and she was cutting grass for the rabbits when somebody called her to come quickly. So she came running and saw her father lying dead on a terrace not far from our house. He was wearing his best waist-coat and he had three thrushes carefully stuffed into one of the top pockets, and it was as if someone had been beside him and had moved him into position, because his legs were straight out in front of him with the toes together, and one arm was along his side, while the other arm lay across his chest, the hand resting just below the little birds. The man who found him said he had not touched him, he had not even gone close because he was so obviously dead.

Agostina could see her father as she told me this; she could see him lying there in the spring sunshine and I could see him too. 'We don't know what happened,' she said, staring into the past. 'We asked people, but no one could tell us.'

---

In June, and I suppose it must have been during the second year of being here, we went to the village square for the festival of Saint Anthony, the desert hermit whose name is given to that illness called shingles, which is known as Saint Anthony's Fire. A bonfire made out of the trunks of big trees had been heaped up in front of the church and it was burning with a steady red heart and scattering sparks like fireflies into the night sky. Trestle tables had been set out with dishes of *focaccia* bread, some covered with a red layer of tomato and a scattering of black olives, and others with onion; there were also slices of salami and big slabs of a flat cake with a crust of sugar on top and numerous bottles of locally made wine, some very vine-gary and some delicious, depending on who had made it and with what grapes. People kept asking if we were now *fissi*, fixed, meaning would we be here for long stretches of time, perhaps even through the winter, and when we said yes, we would be here through the seasons, they said *bravi!* – well done! – as if we had won some sort of prize.

I started a notebook in which I wrote down the names of the people I had met in the village, and the names of their children and other relatives, and where they lived and perhaps something about their appearance. And when the connections became especially complicated I drew a little family tree, with branches dropping down from grandparents and stretching out to include cousins and uncles, brothers and sisters. 'PINO and IDA,' I wrote, and alongside the name of their house I added: 'Two children. Pino was a partisan in the war. He is in his late eighties and not well.'

'MARIO and AGOSTINA: he has a soft face, rosy cheeks and a gentle smile. I think he must have Parkinson's, because his body shakes so much. No car, but a tiny tractor. They have a daughter, but their son died three years ago of a brain tumour and is buried in the cemetery.

NELLA, the postmistress. Same age as me. Reads a lot. She was engaged but he died in 1989.

QUINTO: knows how to build dry-stone walls and his wife LENA has the last cow in the village, which they keep in a shed all through the year. GIOVANIN, the shepherd who brings his sheep past our house in the spring, is Quinto's elder brother.

NANDA, the shopkeeper. Born in 1932. Has never married. Three years older than her sister ADRIANA, who is married to ARTURO. Arturo's youngest son died in a motorcycle accident when he was just seventeen. Two daughters, GABRIELA who lives on the coast and ELIANA who works with her aunt in the shop. Another son called MARCO whom I haven't met. Arturo's mother was LA MUTA, the Silent Woman, and his father was TUNIN THE HUNTER also known as TUNIN DA MUTA.

ARMANDO and CONCETTA: one daughter married to Marco, the other to SERGIO, another of Tunin's grandsons. Armando is Pino's younger brother and they are next door to each other, in the cluster of houses where their parents, uncles and aunts once lived.'

Names were attaching themselves to faces and a whole community was taking shape. Now, if I saw an old man walking along the road carrying a bundle of hay on his back, I could connect him with his wife and his children and his grandchildren. And if I saw Eliana in the shop I could ask her how her mother was doing and what about her sister and her aunt, and when were they planning to harvest the olives and had the wine already been bottled. Quite soon I began to know who lived in each of the houses and in the little walled cemetery I could recognise the family names and from the photographs on the tombstones could see the line of resemblance from one generation to the next. So even though I was still an outsider from a faraway country, I had found a small foothold of belonging.

# Dormice

A family of dormice are sleeping in a crack in the outside wall of our house. I know they are there because I propped a ladder against the wall and climbed up and looked into the depth of grey stone and crumbling cement as soft as icing sugar, and with the help of a torch I could see a breathing bundle of grey fur.

Dormice are very determined hibernators. All through the summer they fill themselves with nuts and fruit and insects and the expanded polystyrene insulation on our water pipe, and the remains of Herman's straw hat and an old leather wallet that got left in the woodshed. Then, when the cold weather comes, they carry their fat bellies into their chosen bedroom and enter a drifting sleep that can last for six or even seven months.

The walls of our house are very thick. I have no idea when it was built, but Agostina says it was abandoned in 1945. Things were terrible at that time. It was the last year of the war, the winter had been bitterly cold, then the chestnut harvest failed and everyone went hungry.

The family who once lived here were called Sasso – an appropriate name in this rocky and stony land since it means stone or rock. There are numerous members of the Rock family buried in the cemetery, along with the Olives and the Cockerels. In the photographs of the deceased printed on china plaques you are confronted by a portrait gallery of this entire village community over the last hundred years and you can see how many of them share the same lean mountain faces and the same stubborn gaze.

When the Sassos decided to sell their house there was not much left of it. The roof and half of the upstairs floor had fallen in, and the window frames were as frail as dried twigs and all their panes of glass had fallen and shattered on the ground. The little dome of a bread oven was clinging to the side of a wall and it still contained the rusting skeleton of the instrument used for sliding out the flat bread made of chestnut flour and a bit of wheat. There was also a big coffin-like storage box and part of a chair and a scythe without a handle and a chain attached to a hook and a broken coffee cup with flowers round its edge.

There was no chimney, but that is not unusual. People had ovens that didn't need chimneys and for the rest they cooked on little cast-iron stoves with a pipe going out of the wall. If they hadn't the money for a stove, they made a fire on stones in a corner of a room and the smoke did its best to escape through holes in the roof, or through an open window.

There were two upstairs rooms. One room was used for drying the chestnuts, which were the staple food for the people here. The chestnuts were laid on wire racks and a fire was lit beneath them and kept burning for several weeks, until the heat had cracked the skins and dried out the dense white flesh. The billowing smoke left yellow and brown stains on the white-washed walls and the flames licked at the roof beams, leaving them black and charred. It must have been a careful balance between preparing the chestnuts and not destroying your house in the process.

The family of Rocks slept in the other room, where we now have a sofa and a desk and a bookcase and no space for much else besides. They probably slept on rickety metal beds and on mattresses that were made of straw stuffed into a sack. And if the family grew larger, it simply meant there was less space for the others, the whole room sighing and muttering with a single voice.

Many creatures have made their home in these walls. Every summer an army of tiny ants emerges from behind a sweet-smelling jasmine bush, which I planted to hide a bit of orange pipe, and they travel to and fro across a battered wooden beam above the back door; perhaps they are in the process of devouring the whole beam, but if so, they are doing it very slowly. For the last couple of years a green lizard with a blue head has been living in a corner where a wall joins a terrace, close to the old path that leads into the woods; on a warm day I see him emerging into the sunlight, his thin fingers drumming on the stones, his tongue flickering to pick up sounds of danger.

One evening we watched a black stream of little bats pouring out from a hole just below the dormice crack and spinning off into the dark sky. We have not seen them since, but perhaps we keep missing the exact moment when they issue forth. Then there is the toad who comes out from her hiding place when it rains and sits by the door as if waiting to be let in. She once woke me out of a deep sleep by knocking the full weight of her body against the door. I went down to see who was there and because I frightened her she raised herself up on stiff legs and made a hissing sound.

And of course we have the dormice. They are the edible dormice, which the ancient Romans used to preserve whole in jars of honey. They are about the same size as squirrels, but with a thinner tail and rounder, more startled eyes. They compensate for their long sleep by indulging in intense activity when they are awake. As soon as they judge the weather to be warm enough they clatter into life. You see them emerging from the crack of their bedroom and clambering across the wall, then with a wild shriek they leap into the thin branches of an oak tree, swinging and tumbling and shrieking some more. Noisy droves of them move among the low trees that grow around the back of our house and when you walk up the track that leads to the road the whole night is alive with the excitement of dormice parties, especially when the moon is full.

Usually you only see the dormice as fleeting silhouettes in the evening light, but once, when I was in our bathroom, I was about to turn on the tap when I became aware of a second and unfamiliar fixture, parallel to the first one. It was grey and motionless, and it took me a few seconds to realise it was a dormouse, with its head pointing down and its tail held straight up along the length of the wall. It kept completely still apart form a slight tremor at the curved tip of its tail, but then I must have moved and the spell was broken and it was gone, scitter-scatter on sharp feet and out of an open window and into the clambering tendrils of the wisteria. I heard it chattering to its friends, telling them the story of a dangerous adventure.

Not long ago we were walking on the Alta Via and were far away from any villages when we met an old man coming towards us along the path through the beech forest. He said he was looking for his cow and he was afraid that the wolves might have got her. He began to talk about the war as if it were still going on; he pointed up at the trees as he described the planes flying overhead and then his face became urgent with fear as he remembered seeing a parachute sailing down from the sky just here; it got tangled in the branches and the man attached to it was killed.

Before continuing on his search for the cow, the man gave us three plums, which he unwrapped from a handkerchief in his pocket, then he was gone. And that night we slept out under the full moon, our sleeping bags nestled on springy grass, in a clearing among the trees. The owls were very busy and every so often there was a swoop of wings quite close to where we lay, and three times we heard a commotion among the leaves and then a shriek as a dormouse was caught by an owl and a diminishing shriek as it was lifted up into the moonlit sky and carried away.

# Insects

This house clings like a solitary beetle to the side of a mountain and there are mountains all around us, although if you look south, you can see the distant triangle of the Mediterranean: sometimes silver and sometimes almost black and sometimes so translucent that there is no horizon drawing a line between the ocean and the sky.

The lower part of the village is beside the river and from our terrace we can see its silver thread, and we can just distinguish the activity of tiny cars and even tinier people on the road: the yellow school bus that stops by the post office at four in the afternoon, the big lorries that bring slate from the mine. And at night there is a white glow from the streetlights and a green glow from the neon sign above Nanda's shop, which is open every day of the year from seven in the morning until nine or even nine thirty at night, apart from Christmas or some important family event like a funeral or a baptism, which means that Nanda is absent for a few hours.

There is also a little village on the slopes of the mountain opposite us and when a flock of sheep and goats is grazing in the steep meadow around the church, they appear as a cluster of white specks. And when the single line of eight streetlights are illuminated, they are like a constellation of stars, suspended in the darkness of the universe.

Three hundred and forty-nine people used to live in that village, but now it is almost completely deserted, with four old women and one old man the only regular inhabitants. There was a fifth woman and we met her once when we were out walking, just a few months before she died. She was coming down the road past some beehives and she was dressed in a girlish cotton frock and accompanied by her grey-haired daughter. We started talking about bees and flowers, and about the robbers who had recently stolen the candlesticks and a figure of the Virgin Mary from the church, when she suddenly said, 'I am ninety-five years old, but I can still dance!' and with that she lifted her arms above her head and did a little pirouette, moving her slippered feet in a quick pattern of steps.

This morning I was looking out at that village and at the rounded outline of a long-since extinct volcano that lies above it. I watched as a plume of clouds swirled around the summit, making it seem as if the volcano had returned to life and was preparing to breathe fire. Further up the valley you can see a much more angular range of tilted limestone strata known as *Pietra Vecchia* or Old Stone. It lies like a vast giant stretched out on his back, his arms clasped over his chest, his eyes closed and his mouth wide open. At the start of the First World War the Alpini Regiment constructed a military road along one side of this mountain; they also cut a footpath that descends the sheer face of the rock. You can still go that way and there are metal rungs and metal handrails to help you where the path is most exposed and the drops most vertical.

We do a lot of walking on the high crests of these mountains. There is a strange sense of freedom that comes from finding yourself so small and insignificant when surrounded by such a rolling immensity of landscape. But then, if you stop and look at the ground beneath your feet, you become aware of all the plants and insects and with that you are suddenly transformed into a huge towering creature.

Early summer is the season for mountain flowers: the creased trumpets of blue gentians and the delicately uncurling heads of purple cyclamen are scattered alongside carpets of violas and pink carnations, solitary lilies and orchids, and clumps of the tall and ghostly asphodel, which are said to grow in the Elysian Fields. And everywhere as you walk, your feet release the oily scent of lavender, rosemary and thyme.

If the weather is warm, dancing butterflies, blue and yellow and white, pose like starlets on the brightest flowers, and armies of crickets and grasshoppers fill the air with their songs of courtship and territory, sounding like tiny lawn sprinklers or helicopters. And if you move in closer you see ants and beetles and the little jumping spiders that leap like panthers on the backs of their prey.

On one walk we came across a thin trickle of water that was issuing out of a stone hut with a wooden door, and when we opened the door we found a little vaulted room that held a shallow pool. I looked at the domed ceiling and at first I thought it was covered with shaggy moss, but then I realised that a twitching carpet of big green crickets was hanging there. They were so shocked by the disturbance that they fell en masse into the water and there was a great thrashing of legs and antennae as they struggled for the shore.

In the local dialect, woodlice are called *babaötti*, the bearded ones, and grasshoppers are *cavalletti*, little horses, and there is a kind of cricket that has its home in the vineyards and only starts to sing when the grapes are ripe and ready to be harvested.

There used to be terrible clouds of flies because everyone lived so close to their animals, often sharing the living space with a flock of goats or a cow. And as well as the flies there were all sorts of other crawling, creeping, jumping, biting, stinging creatures making trouble and if you got bitten the only remedy was to put wet mud on the mark and hope for the best.

In those days there were many more bats at night, jostling crowds of them spinning around the streetlights in the village, and lots of swallows; once every house had a row of swallows' nests, but now there are very few to be seen, although we still have the swifts screaming with a sort of wild excitement as they dive and curve through the element of air. After rain the walls of the terraces were covered with big snails and people would collect them in sacks; now you are more likely to find their traces: clusters of bleached and empty shells that break with the slightest touch.

There are still lots of fireflies. Every evening during the months of June and July, the olive trees and the straggly oaks around our house are pinpricked with their softly winking lights and it's easy to understand how they became the stuff of fairy tales, the will-o'-the-wisps of the south, enticing people to follow their dancing semaphore. 'This way and you will find something you never knew existed. This way and you will be lost for ever.'

When they first appear the fireflies are very bright and purposeful, but as the days move on they lose some of their enthusiasm, the blinking is less frequent and less intense, and they begin to blunder around as if they themselves are lost. They fall into a glass of wine and swim in circles as their lights go dim and gather strength very slowly once they have been saved. They get caught in your hair and land accidentally on an outstretched hand. And when they are really coming to the end of their season they wander around like ordinary brown beetles that happen to have a curious plug fitment on their tail end that occasionally emits a fizzle of light.

---

I like watching insects. I enjoy the perseverance of ants and the doziness of the metallic shield bugs that topple head-first into the white cones of the lilies, to emerge looking drunk, covered in a thick layer of pollen. I can spend ages gazing at the dragonfly nymphs in the water tank shooting out their catapult jaws as they hunt for tadpoles, although I think it's the snake who lives in a hole in the wall who creates such havoc amongst the tadpole population.

Every summer a praying mantis makes his home in a lavender bush, and sits there poised and ready for action, his triangular head swivelling this way and that, his arms bent in supplication and his sharp claws ready to grab and hold. I suppose he wants to catch butterflies, but I have never seen him catch anything even though butterflies often dip dangerously close to him. The lavender bush is also popular with big metallic blue bees that make a lot of noise and fuss and crash into things, and sometimes fall to the ground with their legs thrashing.

I try to be friendly towards wasps and hornets, even though I find hornets unnerving. A group of wasps began to make a paper nest for themselves in the hollow metal pipe that holds up our washing line and when I accidentally knocked against it, one of them whizzed out and stung me on the nose. I also try to be respectful and not too afraid of the black scorpions that are very numerous here, especially in summer.

Scorpions do live outside under stones, or in bits of old wood, but they seem to prefer the comfort and security of a house. They find dark hiding places behind a picture on the wall, or in the crack of a wooden beam, and they stay quiet all through the day and go hunting at night. You suddenly become aware of the unmistakable silhouette of a scorpion on a white expanse of wall, or see one of them making a leisurely journey across the ceiling. For a while we had an especially large representative of the species living behind the water cistern in the bathroom. You'd go in and put on the light just in time to witness that prehistoric, jointed, shiny, pincer-fronted, arrow-tailed creature of nightmares, sliding carefully back into his safe hiding place between the wall and the white plastic of the tank. I try to not talk aloud to myself too often, but I notice that I do say things to the scorpions: words of supplication and prayers that they might leave me in peace, although I'm not sure which part of their jointed anatomy they use for the purpose of listening.

The insects here can be very large. The caterpillar of the goat moth is as big as a cigar and looks as if it has been stitched together out of pieces of fur and leather. We had a hairy, fawn-coloured drinker moth that rested on a wall in the sunshine for half a day, and we made a photograph of it next to a ruler in case we forgot its true size. Recently I found the wing of a giant peacock moth lying on the road and it was as big as half a postcard, covered with an intricate silken pattern of soft reds and browns with a single wild staring eye. But the biggest of them all was a beetle.

I was on my own here and although I told myself that I wasn't nervous of the darkness of the woodshed or the rustling of unseen creatures among the trees, I did notice that I was rather awkward and hasty in my movements and I went to bed very early.

I was woken by what sounded like venetian blinds being rattled at the window, and since we have no venetian blinds, I tried to work out what else it might be. Bamboo canes in the wind perhaps, but there was no wind and no bamboo.

I waited, more mystified than afraid. The rattling stopped and was replaced by a metallic fluttering followed by a rustling close to my ear and by then I had put on the light.

There, lying on the pillow next to where my head had been, was a beetle as big as my hand. He was a dull beige colour, with a narrow body and very long antennae. He sat there completely still, antennae waving.

There was something so awkward and apologetic in his manner that I said, 'Oh, hello!' as if I wanted to reassure him. Then I got up and very gently lifted the pillow on which he was perched and took it and him to the open window. I gave the pillow a little shake, which made him cling on all the more tightly, but after a while he tried lifting one hooked foot and then another, like an impatient horse, and suddenly, without a backward glance or a word of thanks, he launched his improbable body into the night and was gone.

# Caves

Apart from the volcano, the mountains here are all made from limestone. I learnt it at school: how sand and mud and bits of marine life turned into rocky sediment under the weight of the Sea of Thetis. Then there was a great rumbling in the belly of the earth and a great shifting of the tectonic plates, and the sea vanished and the rocks buckled and reared up and here we are. Simply put, but you can see it sometimes: the stripy layers of rock pushed into such unlikely and precarious angles and still so vivid with energy it's as if this is just a lull and they are about to get back to their grinding and crashing movements within the next moment.

I also learnt about limestone and what happens when water seeps in through the cracks and dissolves the rock so that caves and passageways and deep holes are formed, along with stalactites and stalagmites and smooth surfaces that gleam like melted wax.

The first human beings came to live in some of these caves and they used others as burial places for the bodies of their dead. All along this part of the coast and inland as far as the high village where the shepherds lived, you find evidence of this human past. Smoke stains from fires. Little piles of bears' teeth kept as trophies, perhaps to show who won the fight. Fragments of animal bones, split open to reach the marrow: wild pig and wild ox and a type of red deer known by its Latin name as *pudus pendulus*. Mounds of seashells, limpets mostly, some of them pierced. Worked flakes of flint. The vertebrae of salmon and trout, which were good for making into necklaces.

The skeleton of a woman lies on her back and her body is covered by a blanket of thousands of little *trochus* shells. A pebble painted red is under her head and the jawbones of two very young children are there with her, also covered by shells. She is of the Cro-Magnon race and fifty thousand years have passed since she died.

Another cave and a trench have been filled with the red stain of iron oxide, which must have been brought here from far away. Three skeletons

lie close together, like seeds in a pod. A very tall young man, his head turned to the left, looks out towards the west where the sun sets over the sea. He wears a necklace made from deer teeth, salmon vertebrae and pieces of ivory, all marked with little carved incisions. A larger piece of ivory shaped like a double olive is on his chest; it must have been for fastening his cloak, but the cloak has vanished. Two pierced cowrie shells are placed one on each side of his left knee. A well-worked flint knife is in easy reach of his left hand.

A young woman lies on her side next to him, her head propped on the femur of an ox. One arm is bent, so that her hand touches her chin, while the hand of the other bent arm holds a flint knife. A little double olive of ivory is on her chest as well and a crown of shells and fish vertebrae is on her head. Beside her, so close he seems to be clinging to her for comfort, is a teenage boy. His head lies on a flint scraper, his left hand is under his chin. He wears a necklace made from teeth and bones and a skullcap made from perforated shells and fish vertebrae. His ivory cloak fastener has slipped to one side so that it lies on the red ground near his hand.

There is a similar burial cave from a later period, close to where the river from our valley reaches the sea. It's in the middle of a sprawling town that grows bigger every year, not far from the Martello tower used by Napoleon when he was here with his armies and also not far from the ice-cream parlours and the shops selling Levi jeans, and the concrete muddle of new apartment blocks and the noise and clutter of cars and the drift of modern dust and rubbish. The cave is closed to visitors and the bones it contained were handed over to a local museum, but now nobody seems to know where they are.

If you go by car all the way from the mouth of the river to the head of the valley, the journey will take you about an hour and a quarter just so long as you don't get stuck for too long behind one of the little motorbike tractors named *ape* or *vespa* because of the fierce wasp- or bee-buzzing of their engines. A man and perhaps his wife and child and even the dog are squashed into the front seat, and they look hunched and stubborn, maybe because they know they can't go any faster and there is a long line of traffic behind them.

You go through the first of two narrow gorges at a place called Campo Marzio. There's a metal sign fixed to the wall by the road and if you look up you can see the fragmented remains of a fortress clinging like a limpet to an escarpment of rock. I was told it was built in 181 BC to celebrate the Roman conquest of the wild Ligurian tribes who were getting in the way of the colonising process. The war had lasted for more than a hundred years and although the Ligurians were officially defeated, many of them had simply escaped to the higher land where they hid in some of the same deep caves that their distant ancestors had used. According to Pliny the Elder, the Roman soldiers would search for these caves and wall them up and light a fire at the entrance with the occupants trapped inside. In more recent times the partisans who were hiding from the Fascists used the same caves, lit fires where fires had been lit before, and when they uncovered old bones, moved them to one side.

After the fortress gate, the road follows the flank of the mountains and takes you to a big village. Dark medieval alleyways are piled up behind a noisy modern main street and there is a fierceness to the people who live here. The men tend to look drunk and rumpled at all times of the day and the two dark and beautiful women who serve in the little supermarket use the most vivid obscenities as part of their ordinary speech. They curse the weather with the stinking bollocks of Christ and make jokes about sexual organs while selling green peppers and yellow bananas.

The cave known as *Tana Bertrand* – Bertrand's Lair – is above this village. It used to be a walk of an hour and a half to get there, but the hunters don't keep the path open any longer and it's very hard to find. There are old stories of a great battle that was fought close to the cave and that is why it is still haunted, the ghosts of the dead wailing and milling about at night, carrying dim lights.

*Tana Bertrand* was explored in the early part of the last century by an intrepid Englishwoman called Grace Crowfoot who was looking for a rare variety of blind beetle that made its home in dark places. The village priest was a friend of hers and people from the village led her to the cave. The entrance was only four feet high and it was filled with earth and the rubble of fallen stones. Beyond it was a long low tunnel, which widened out into a second and much larger cave.

On her first visit in 1908 and before she had even begun to look for the beetles, Grace Crowfoot came across two human jawbones and a human thigh bone. Over several months she spent a total of thirty-one days scrabbling away in dark and cramped conditions. She found her beetles, more human bones, two little carved female figures, a necklace made from shells and salmon vertebrae and some flint tools. She showed these treasures to her friend Professor Lessi, who knew about such things and he said the bones were Paleolithic, dating from 25,000 BC, and because there were no signs of a fire having been lit he decided the cave had been used for burial purposes only. There was evidence of other human occupation over the years and perhaps even the partisans were here for a while, their faces blotched and sore from eating too many raw chestnuts and not enough of anything else.

Armando, who lives down the road in the house of his childhood, told me how he was out hunting not long after the war and he crossed over a wooden plank somewhere in the mountains close to the border with France and it led him to a deep cave; inside the cave there was a heap of bones. At first he thought they were the bones of a chamois but then he saw the long leg bones and the broken human skull of what he called *un buon Cristiano*, although I suppose it could well have been the remains of someone who had lived and died long before the birth of Christ.

# Wild Pigs

A narrow path leads from our house, up through the olive groves and into the chestnut forests. Foxes and shambling badgers and polecats live there, as well as all sorts of little mice and birds, and sometimes you might come across that mysterious creature called a fire salamander, pretending to be dead for safety's sake, eyes open but unblinking; its lizard body is as black as a dustbin bag and splashed with patches of brilliant yellow. But the real lords of these forests are the wild pigs. You see signs of them everywhere: the sharp print of their feet; areas of ground they have ploughed with their powerful noses; little mudbaths where they wallow on a hot day; and the steep tunnelling tracks through the undergrowth that they use like chutes when they need to escape in a hurry.

The wild pigs are not dangerous – unless they happen to feel threatened or cornered – and they keep to themselves through most of the year. But in the spring when they have their young to feed, and especially if the weather has been bad, hunger makes them brave and they come to the villages for a little light scavenging. They use their bulldozer bodies to break through fences into gardens and vineyards and create havoc, rooting up potatoes, tearing at new vine shoots and trampling on every lettuce and parsley seedling they can find.

We sometimes hear the wild pigs at night, grunting and snorting quite close to the house. Once, when I was driving home along the track, I surprised a family of three stripy babies and their heavy mother. When I stopped, they stopped too, caught in the headlights of the car, before scattering out of sight. And then there was the evening when we were sitting on the terrace and I glanced up to see an enormous boar gazing down at me from just a few yards away. He didn't look aggressive, but then again, nor did he look shy, and there was something proprietorial in his manner, as if we were intruders on his land. Our fox terrier saw him as well, but instead of barking or making some other acknowledgement of this alien visitor, she just stared in silent amazement. I must have looked away for a moment and when I looked back the boar had melted into the darkness.

There was a time when these chestnut forests were kept in very good order. The old trees with their huge reptilian trunks were carefully pruned and lopped of dead branches. The ground beneath them was raked and cleared to make way for a thin crop of grass, and all through the months of September, October and November whole families went to live there, busy with the work of harvesting the chestnuts.

Most people here couldn't afford the luxury of a mule, so they set out on foot, taking everything they needed. The women carried big baskets balanced on their heads, filled with provisions; if there was a baby it would be placed there too, swaddled like a chrysalis. The men had containers strapped round the waist and across the forehead to balance the weight and they carried tools and more essentials of dried food: pasta, flour, sugar and a wheat grain that could be roasted and made into a sort of coffee. They also brought empty sacks for the chestnuts, and saucepans, buckets, tin mugs and dishes, knives and spoons, and perhaps a piece of soap and some rags that could be useful in all sorts of ways.

The houses they occupied were small and simple. The stone walls were not cemented on the outside or plastered on the inside. Families slept together on beds of dried grass. They cooked on an open fire, ate at a table made from rough slices of chestnut wood and sat on chairs that were grey boulders. The first task of the morning was to collect water from the nearest spring or little stream and that often meant a steep walk of an hour or more; but the real work was the chestnuts. The spiky fruit was collected with bare hands and brought to a pounding floor where they were thumped with an instrument called an *apanca*, which looks like a big wooden mushroom with nails hammered into its round cap.

Today, if you walk through the forests, you come across what is left of the old houses, but they are now so derelict they look like part of the natural landscape. Low clusters of stone crouch under the looming trees that surge around their walls and push new saplings through collapsed roofs and across open doorways. The *padroni* – the almost feudal landlords – are long since dead and nobody cares who owns these trees that are as battered as the houses, while the forest floor, which was once kept as clean and neat as a front parlour, is a jumble of broken branches and fallen trunks.

Since the chestnuts are no longer being collected and carried away, the wild pigs can claim everything as their own, and they eat to their hearts' content and grow fat and multiply.

So now the hunting season has replaced the season of harvesting and every Wednesday and Sunday from September to December the hunters go in search of the chestnut eaters. They form squadrons of some twenty or thirty men, and have big rifles and camouflage costumes and walkie-talkies, and they are bound by all sorts of rules and regulations.

Each squadron is responsible for a couple of packs of loose-bodied hunting dogs, their enormous splayed feet designed to take them safely down pig chutes. When these dogs are on a scent they produce an echoing, gurgling cry that reverberates around the whole valley and they often get so excited by the chase that they forget their owners and run off into the forest for days on end.

One dog arrived here in the middle of the night. We heard the clanking of his bell and he howled to be let in, but when we opened the door for him he let out another howl and ran away. He was back in the morning, and he dipped and wriggled and rolled on his belly to show his appreciation when we gave him some food, and let us read the telephone number on his collar so we could contact his owner.

Sometimes the squadron returns empty handed and sometimes it returns triumphant and sometimes, with that curious human mixture of savagery and compassion, the squadron returns with a wild pig orphan in need of care and protection until it is big enough to be sent back to find its friends and relations in the forest.

---

Maria and Quinto had a baby wild pig living with them last December. They called it Cinghialetto, which just means 'baby wild pig' although the name sounds like a carillon of little bells.

When I first saw Cinghialetto, he was no bigger than a loaf of bread; his sorrowful dark-rimmed eyes were fringed with absurdly long lashes and his bristly coat was patterned like a hairdresser's dream of glamour in stripes of orange and black and platinum blond. But even then he already had a very grown-up smell of wildness.

34

Cinghialetto had been given an old wooden crate filled with disposable nappies to sleep in, and at first he lived in Maria and Quinto's kitchen, where he skittered around the television set and sniffed at the feet of visitors who came to drink some of Quinto's terrible red wine, which gives you a headache even before you have finished one small glass of the stuff. Maria was feeding this new baby six times a day with a mixture of milk and eggs and sweet biscuits, which she put into a beer bottle with a teat. He skittered after her wherever she went, butting into her legs and nibbling at the toes of her slippers.

After a few weeks Cinghialetto's box was placed under a table on the terrace with a plastic cloth hanging down to provide a bit of privacy, but he was always waiting for a chance to thunder back into the kitchen. And when Maria felt he was ready to be weaned, he made a dreadful fuss, producing an hysterical pig-scream all through the night and knocking over his food dish, which Maria had filled with pasta, pieces of cheese rind and old apples and tomatoes. He still skittered after her, but she had to be careful of the thudding weight of his body against her legs and she pushed him away when he bit her slippers.

Then Quinto was ill and it was all too much, so Cinghialetto went to live further up the mountain, with a man called Ginetto. Cinghialetto now has a little house and a paddock all to himself and he screams a wild-pig welcome when he sees Ginetto, rolling over on his back with his eyes closed to have his tummy scratched. He will be set free, but not until this year's hunting season is over.

---

In a village further up the valley they have a five-year-old wild pig. She weighs over one hundred and fifty kilos and her name is Zerba. Zerba lives in a little stall, which used to house the goats, and she spends her days in a somnambulant dream, staring through the bars of her door. But every so often she is let out and then she can walk down to the spring and play in the mud and find chestnuts and have fun. The couple who own her have barricaded the road with some old bed frames, just in case she thinks of escaping.

We had seen Zerba a few times, her long and somehow prehistoric face peering through the bars of her cage. We would give her some grass or a few chestnuts and inhale her wild-pig stink, which was strong enough to make you sneeze. And then one day when we were coming back from a walk in the mountains, we met a man who said, 'Come and meet Zerba. She is with my wife enjoying the afternoon sunshine. Don't be afraid, she's as gentle as a baby.'

And there she was, a wild animal made tame, ambling with the woman up the narrow path from the spring. It was a lovely sight.

'Hello, Zerba,' we said. I gave her a few chestnuts from my pocket and she nuzzled for more, a little roughly I thought, but never mind.

She also nuzzled a little roughly against my son's leg, but still her owner smiled and called her *Amore*, and everything was fine.

Zerba was just ahead of us when she suddenly stopped and stared, with that same proprietorial air as the boar I had seen near the terrace.

At that moment some ancient switch was pulled and she charged us. She knocked Herman over with one butt of her huge head; our son rushed forward to save his stepfather and not knowing what else to do, he grabbed hold of Zerba by both of her bristly ears. 'Oh, Zerba, *Amore!*' cried the woman imploringly, and she called for her husband to come quickly, but there was no answering call.

Our son was still holding Zerba's ears and my husband was back on his feet, but we were all at a loss about what to do next. Without having a clear plan I picked up a piece of wood and bashed it on Zerba's head. She paused and looked slightly surprised, and as luck would have it her owner arrived at that moment; with a few words of reassurance, he persuaded Zerba to return quietly to her stall.

On our way home we stopped at a café and as we came through the door a little dog approached us, sniffed at our clothes and began dancing in wild circles round our feet. We realised that we stank of wild pig and that was why the little dog was so delighted to make our acquaintance.

# Following the Road

Even before the last war, there was a paved road that more or less followed the line of the river from the coast as far as the next village from ours, the one where they used to have ten water mills grinding wheat for flour. A horsedrawn carriage brought the post once a day and also carried people if they needed to be carried. The carriage was replaced by a rickety bus, which fell off a bridge one bitterly cold night in February 1920, when it was bringing everyone back from a fair. Twenty-three of them were drowned in the icy water.

And then the war came to the valley and there was the unfamiliar noise of many engines churning away as long lines of jeeps and lorries arrived with their loads of soldiers and weaponry. So the road became a crucial part of the war and its bridges were blown up and hand grenades were thrown at it and people watched from their houses or their hiding places to see what was going to happen next. When they were desperate during the winter of 1944 and the spring of 1945, some of the women were brave enough to walk along the road as far as the coast carrying metal containers on their backs, which they filled with seawater because no one had any salt for cooking.

After the war the bridges were repaired or replaced, the potholes were mended and people returned to a changed but continuing way of life, and the road was extended as far as the medieval town halfway up the valley. But there it stopped. If you wanted to go to the end of the valley as far as the village that was destroyed by an avalanche you had to go on foot or with a mule.

It was the same for all the other villages: the ones that clung on the slopes of the mountains, and the ones that were perched like a cluster of little birds on a summit. They could only be approached via an intricate geometry of footpaths or on the old mule tracks, which cross arched stone bridges with not enough room on them for two people to stand side by side and follow slanting cobbled steps, the stones worn smooth by the passing of so many feet.

Each house, each tiny building, was the heart at the centre of its own network of arteries and veins. This way and you will reach a spring for water; that way will take you past a patch of trees where porcini mushrooms are often found; if you continue you come to a clearing where the chalk burners sleep and make their annual pyramids of fire. Up further and here are the huts used during the chestnut harvest; further still and this is where people came during the summer months and now you are approaching the crest of the mountains: the landscape of the shepherds and their flocks.

Everyone was isolated within their own small communities. A village that could be clearly seen on the opposite slope of the mountain could only be reached after a five-hour walk; it must have seemed like a foreign country where the inhabitants had different habits, different jokes and stories, different ways of preparing ravioli and even a different language. Lena in our village will call a sheep a *fea*, but only three miles away the same shaggy creature has metamorphosed into a *pegue*. The rain that falls on our house is *bavaia*, but the same rain a little further up the valley has turned into *pioviggima*. Eliana says that old people sometimes come into the shop and ask for something using a dialect word she has never heard before; they don't know what it might be in Italian, so it's a question of guesswork.

When we wanted to find our way around on the old paths, we began by using the military maps that were produced in the 1930s, but although they show the steepness of a mountain or the direction taken by a little stream, they don't allow for the fact of landslides or the determination of bushes and young saplings to wipe out all evidence of people having passed this way before. Even the more recent maps seem to rely on the old ones and modern guidebooks only describe the most obvious routes that have been marked with cairns or painted dots and stripes.

We kept trying to work out how to get from our house to the lower village following a path that was once marked with seven wooden crosses along the way. One of the crosses is planted on the rocks above a cliff, in a place called the Rock of the Cross which is close to us. From this point you can look up at a tiny scattering of houses where people came in the summer. The lavender pickers were there as well and I was told that they all slept in a barn filled with hay and the woman who cooked

food for them in the evening made a tomato sauce for the pasta, for which she chewed up cloves of garlic and spat them one by one into a big pot.

The cliff edge is a sheer drop and fat little sand martins and thin screaming swifts come swooping in on the updraft, sometimes so close that their feathers almost brush against your face. A pair of peregrine falcons have their nest a little way along from here and sometimes you see one of them billowing into the air, the sharp yellow of their legs clearly visible as they release their curious yelping cry. And it was here that I saw a raven holding a twig in its beak and the twig was turning like a little propeller.

———————————•———————————

We were at the Rock of the Cross when we met a tall shy man who said he was taking the path to the lower village and we asked if we could follow him. He plunged ahead while we did our best to keep up with him, struggling like ducklings following their mother. When we were in sight of the road he stopped, checking to see if we were following, and disappeared, but we reached our destination feeling triumphant. A few days later we tried to go the same way again, but we got lost close to some ruined houses we had never seen before and after thrashing about for a while we had to give up and return home.

But in spite of such failures, a series of intricate little maps was beginning to take shape inside our minds. We learnt to anticipate the crucial turning close to a curiously square-shaped boulder on the way to the high pastures and from there we could zigzag through the chestnut forest, recognising the ruined shells of buildings along the way. We knew how to emerge above the treeline at the place where a little altar has been set up among a scattering of pink-coloured slates and from there we could find the path that leads to the crest of the mountains facing our house. Once we were there, we could find our way home again without searching for empty beer cans or other vague signs of civilisation. 'Ah, here we are,' we'd say when we reached the wall of a ruined building with a coffee cup hanging from a hook. 'Ah, here we are,' at the door of a tiny hut with the date 1886 carved on the stone lintel above the entrance. Slowly we were becoming surrounded by familiar hieroglyphs and with that the mountains became less huge and the forests less dense.

We'd tell the old people where we had been. '*Santa Madonna!* You went there?' said Agostina, her eyes widening, her hand to her mouth to show her amazement. 'I used to go that way every day in summer when I was a girl. Maybe you saw our house. The track was made for mules who carried the chestnuts, the wine, the lavender. You cross the stream by the pool where we washed our clothes and then you know you are close when you reach the big rock that was always blue with lavender. Someone used a knife to cut the name Pipa on the wall of our house. Maybe you saw that. *Santa Madonna*, I hope there were no snakes!'

The road finally made its way to the end of the valley in 1972 and, in a great flurry of building work, other roads were being built at the same time, tarmac or concrete constructions that took no notice of the tight little corners made by the mule tracks but swept forward in great hairpin bends. People watched amazed as the door to the outside world was flung open, while at the same time the many little doors and passageways to the world all around them seemed quietly to swing shut because they had lost their importance, their dignity of purpose.

The bustling and round-bodied woman who runs the café at the second gorge, where the valley is flanked on either side by steep curtains of yellow and orange limestone, remembers the drama of the arrival of the new road. She says her house was in a meadow and there were steep terraces all the way down to the river far below. She heard the roar of the bulldozers approaching and then there they were and they tore up the meadow round her house with such ease. She found it wonderful to watch them. 'It was the most exciting thing that had ever happened in my life,' she said, a little embarrassed by the thought.

Next they built the suspension bridge, which started as a complicated skeleton of metal stretching out step by step over the gorge and was transformed into an elegant concrete body that leapt like a hare from one side to the other. The people from the village on the other side who had mostly kept to themselves for as long as they could remember, approached in a nervous little crowd to watch this transformation. They stood there in a daze because regardless of what else might happen, they knew that from this moment nothing would ever be the same again.

# Sheep and Goats

In February or early March, depending on the weather, Giovanin the shepherd begins to move his flock of sheep and goats back to the high mountain pastures. He sets out from his winter house, which is the house where he was born seventy-three years ago, and follows a steep path down into a little river valley, over a humped bridge that is said to have been built by the Romans and up the other side through the forest. This is the way the children from his village used to come to school every morning, each one carrying a log for the classroom fire during the winter. The winters can be very cold here, with ice on the ground and canopies of snow ready to drop from the branches of the trees.

Giovanin doesn't take his flock all the way into the church square, where the old people once sat on benches under the shade of two horse chestnuts, moving rosary beads between their fingers as they talked about the small details of village life. Instead, to avoid any encounters with cars and people, he takes a much more complicated route that zigzags close to the edge of a precipitous cliff and finally emerges among the olive groves just below our terrace. We know when he is passing because we are woken in the early morning by the clanking of bells.

Giovanin has eighty sheep and ten goats, although he used to have twice that number. At this time of the year his sheep are still very shaggy and their yellowish-grey wool is twisted into long dreadlocks. Their bony naked heads are sculpted into an angular hump from nostril to forehead, which makes them look like members of an ancient and noble tribe. They tend to be silent with none of the restless 'Where? Here! There!' uncertainties of their more northern relatives. The goats are also quiet. Their coats are sleek and their horns are long and they have an expression of permanent surprise on their soft faces.

The bells clank as the animals graze on the tough grass between the olive trees; Giovanin stands close by, watching them. Sometimes he might sit on a rock and watch them from this different vantage point and sometimes his gaze is briefly diverted, while he looks up at the sky or at the high ridge of the mountains.

He is accompanied by three dogs who are covered with so much long, coarse and weather-resistant hair that it's hard to see their faces. Lupo, the leader, would have no problem chasing off any wolf that dared to approach his sheep with a hungry look in its eyes. Bruno and Fabri are smaller and with less of an air of grim authority. Their job is to keep the flock compact and well ordered, and although Giovanin rarely gives them any instructions they are always on the move, gently arranging and rearranging the sheep while Lupo watches them and does nothing to help.

Whenever our scatty fox terrier meets up with Giovanin's three dogs, she is on her very best behaviour. She lowers her head and her tail as a sign of submission and waits for them to inspect her, which they do with all the bureaucratic thoroughness of customs officials at a difficult border crossing. She even keeps very still if a big sheep comes sidling up and nudges against her with its humped nose. She is conscious that her every move is being observed and assessed, and she must make no mistakes.

Shepherds take great pride in their dogs. I was told of a shepherd called Luigi who lives further up the valley, who says that his dog has more wisdom and good sense than any human being he has met, and in honour of this fact he invites the dog to share lunch with him every Sunday. So the two of them sit side by side at the kitchen table and have a dish of pasta, with perhaps a nice bit of sausage lurking in the tomato sauce.

Giovanin stays in the olive groves only for as long as it takes for his animals to eat the best of the grass. Then he is on his way, following a path that briefly crosses the road and threads up to Adriana's tiny village.

Adriana owns the forest above her house and it is maintained like no other I have seen. Every spring they prune the trees and rake up great heaps of brown leaves and spiky husks and burn them, so that the trees look pleased with themselves, while the ground beneath them is like a well-swept green carpet. Giovanin's sheep graze here for a month, before moving on. He always presents Adriana with a bowl of ricotta by way of thanks.

I was talking to Nella, who runs the village post office. We are the same age and she reads a lot and is very well informed about novels and academic studies that deal with the war and its aftermath. She recently told me about her father, who also worked in the post office, and how he was accused of being a Fascist, even though he couldn't bear anything to do with politics and always tried to keep to himself as much as possible. He had been a soldier in the Abyssinian campaign of 1935 and had witnessed some terrible things that made him cry, although he could never speak of them. When Nella was a child she often asked him what had happened, but all he would say was that the sun was so hot in the desert you could fry an egg on a stone. Then he would return to silence. One day in 1958 Nella walked into the family kitchen and found him lying on the floor covered in blood because he had just tried to kill himself with a knife. His job at the post office came to an abrupt end and he was sent to a hospital several hundred miles away. Nella visited him whenever she could. The doctors told her not to say anything that might upset him and so she never mentioned the death of his wife, her mother, or any of the other things that were going on in the village he had left behind.

Anyway, Nella was telling me that when Giovanin was a young man, all the girls longed to marry him because he was so beautiful. 'But don't say I told you!' she says. 'He is very shy and it would embarrass him.'

She explains that shepherds are like a different race of people because they have chosen such a solitary existence; even when Giovanin was a little boy he was cut off from the other children and knew he wanted to be a shepherd. By the time he was fourteen he was up in the mountains for months on end. So in spite of his beauty he remained single because there were few girls who would want to share such a life.

I have often walked passed Giovanin's winter house. It's at the end of a long track. It has a sagging electric line that looks as though it might be used to hang out the washing and there is a plastic pipe that brings a trickle of water from a nearby spring. But the place is beautiful in its remoteness and there are cherry trees and apple trees and a little vineyard and a vegetable bed where flowers grow among bedraggled leeks and cabbages. A tiny tractor is usually parked by the wood pile and it is covered with a sheet of blue plastic, which in turn is covered with the brindled hide of a cow, tied in place with a length of rope, making the tractor look as if it is caught in the act of metamorphosis – half machine, half animal.

I have also seen Giovanin's house in the mountains. It's set on a steep slope littered with rocks and boulders. It has no soil for a garden and no electricity, although Giovanin recently acquired a solar panel, which provides enough energy for a couple of light bulbs, and he grows a few tomato plants in a plastic grow-bag by the door.

He and his flock and the three dogs are out every day. They go from the Pass of the Dish to the Place of the Standing Stone to the gently sloping Pass of the Half Moon; on all sides the mountains roll into the far distance like the waves of a petrified sea. He needs to move around a lot in search of good pasture and when he is too far away to get back to his hut at night he sleeps in one of the low stone shelters built by generations of shepherds with just enough space for a single supine body, while the dogs watch over his flock. If there is no shelter nearby he makes himself a bivouac from the plastic sheet he carries with him.

He is out every day in the thin air, a big cloth tied like a turban round his head, and he carries a cloth bag that must contain the plastic sheet and a bit of food and water. I have seen him sitting quietly on a rock during a rainstorm, his clothes soaking wet, and I have seen him in the far distance moving slowly across the rolling waves of the landscape, his flock milling and scattering on all sides.

There are hares in the mountains, although not many are left since people stopped cultivating the terraced fields of wheat the hares liked so much. But the pretty chamois with their striped faces and little horns like the handles of a lady's umbrella are increasing in numbers. Wolves are coming back and there are also a few wild goats, their heads bent under the weight of their huge arched horns. Sometimes Giovanin might see a marmot, perched on its fat bottom like a giant guinea pig, and if he doesn't see it he will hear it whistling to its friends with the same shrill cry of someone whistling for a taxi in a crowded street.

# Fragility

Four years went by. The wisteria now waved its long tendrils into the open window of the upstairs bedroom and seemed intent on taking complete possession of the house. During a thunderstorm I had witnessed a green lightning ball bouncing across the kitchen like a special effect in a Hollywood movie; it burst the life out of the telephone and the CD player with a brief crackling sound as if they had been shot in the heart. Then it was gone, leaving the acrid stink of burnt electric wires as a souvenir of its passing.

I had found a lizard that had made its home in one of the pockets of the case of my laptop and I had counted twenty-five little bats emerging out of a hole in the wall. I could recognise the cry of the Uhu owl ever since the night one of them flew close by the open bedroom window and woke us with the clear enunciation of its name. I knew how to pickle olives in salty water and I had come to expect the arrival of the fireflies in early June, along with the occasional miraculous visitation of a hoopoe. People here call the hoopoe the May Hen, which makes it sound very ordinary and doesn't do any justice to the soft pink of its breast feathers, the thin curving beak and the black-and-white speckled crown on its head that opens and closes like a fan.

Quite early one morning – it must have been towards the beginning of June – we met Marco, Arturo and Adriana's eldest son. His three shaggy hunting dogs came bounding down on to our terrace and greeted us like old friends; then he emerged out of the forest from the same place where I had seen the wild boar. He was a tall, handsome man with a round face and a soft voice, and he wore a blue cotton handkerchief tied tight round his head, like a pirate. He was easygoing and friendly, and he sat in the sunshine and talked with us, eager to practise the English he had learnt when he was working in a hotel on the coast. He said that since coming back to live in the village a short while ago, his sense of what was important in life had changed completely. Now all that he wanted was to work on the land that belonged to his family and to walk in the mountains.

We made a pot of Lapsang Souchong tea, which he had never tasted before, and he liked it very much, trying to find the words to describe its smoky flavour. Then he got to his feet and thanked us, called his dogs and was gone, back into the forest. It was only later that we learnt he had previously been very ill with cancer and, after a spell of remission, the cancer had returned with a new vehemence. He had just finished a course of chemotherapy, which was why he was wearing the pirate's handkerchief, to hide the bald patches on his head.

A few days after this Herman had gone to do something with the car and I was standing in the kitchen when I heard a loud bang of metal on metal. I rushed outside just in time to see the car leaping over the unfenced edge of the parking space and nosediving some twenty feet towards the terraces below. There was an even louder bang as it landed. I ran out and down the steps towards the car, terrified of what I might see when I got there.

'I'm all right, I'm all right,' he was calling to me, and I found him curled up in a nest of broken windscreen glass and thin branches. The dented body of the car was a few feet away, leaning its underbelly against the trunk of the olive tree, which had stopped its bouncing descent.

He said he thought nothing was broken. He explained that he had wanted to move the car but had no ignition key with him so he had let it roll forward and then of course the brakes didn't work, which he should have known but somehow forgot, and the car hit the red oil drum filled with flowers, but that didn't stop it and we still hadn't got a metal railing installed and by then it was too late to do anything. He had managed to roll out when the door on the driver's side flew open and he had landed well because he was always good at landing well. He said that although he was sure it was nothing really serious, his left shoulder was beginning to hurt a lot.

I sat with him for a while, then helped him make the slow ascent to the house; this was probably the wrong thing to do but never mind, we did it all the same. Once he was inside and lying on the sofa he went pale and ice cold and began to shiver. I called friends who contacted the emergency services and within half an hour an ambulance was coming cautiously down our track, its blue lights flashing. Herman was checked over by three men and a woman in uniform, then they strapped him to a stretcher and drove him to the nearest hospital.

The doctors took X-rays of his skull and his spine and examined him from head to toe. They said he had broken his collarbone and had perhaps cracked a couple of ribs, but it could have been so much worse. They fitted him with a harness to keep his shoulder immobile and gave him a packet of strong painkillers, and he was free to go home.

Over the next few days several people from the village came to look at the car lying on its side close to the trunk of the olive tree, the broken glass from the windscreen glinting in the sunshine. They also wanted to take a look at the man who had made such a leap and survived. 'You must have a good guardian angel,' said Agostina, and crossed herself because of the miracle.

On 10 July, during that same intense bundle of time, we were invited to celebrate the fiftieth wedding anniversary of Adriana and her husband Arturo. A service was held in the church in the lower village and it was packed with people from all over the valley. The old couple sat side by side in the front row, their shoulders touching, and they listened with serious faces to the words of the priest and joined in with the echoing prayers of the congregation. At a certain point someone called for them to kiss, so they stood up shyly and turned towards each other like a groom and his new bride, and their lips briefly met and everyone clapped. Their son Marco was there with his own son and his baby girl and his pretty wife, but by now he was very weak, his face swollen because of the treatment he had been receiving.

We had to go to England for a few weeks and while we were away we received a black-bordered envelope with a postmark from the village. We thought it must be bad news about Marco, but instead it was his father Arturo. His car had also slipped over an unfenced edge and had plunged down to the terrace below, but he had not been as lucky as Herman and the fall killed him. His funeral had already taken place by the time we got the letter.

We arrived back on 20 November. Marco was being cared for by all the members of his family. Everyone in the village looked exhausted, their eyes haunted by this new tragedy that was moving closer step by step. He died on 8 December and was buried two days later, close to the fresh grave of his father and the much older grave of his younger brother. The same people who had come to celebrate the wedding anniversary were here again to say farewell. The slow procession of mourners moved like a stream along the road towards the cemetery and the police were there to hold up the traffic until everyone had passed.

I caught sight of Adriana: tiny and fierce and despairing and flanked by her two daughters, who each held her by an arm because otherwise she would have fallen over. I was walking with Herman and Nella from the post office was next to me. She and I held hands as the burden of flowers was lifted from the coffin. It was midday.

That evening we had a phone call. We were already upstairs and in bed when I heard the solemn urgency of a voice speaking into the answering machine. I went down to listen to the message.

A young woman whom I had known since she was two years old, who had been like my first daughter and whom my children saw as their half-sister and sometimes even their younger mother, had died in an absurd accident at eleven in the morning, UK time. She had been dying as I was walking to the cemetery in a river of people and by the time Marco's coffin was entering the hard earth she was already dead.

I told Nanda and Eliana in the shop that I had to go quickly to England and when I told them why they nodded their heads and stared at me with sad eyes. Nella, whose father had gone mad and whose friend had died when he might have lived, was in the shop as well. The news travelled around the village.

I went on my own to meet up with my children and then Herman came to join me a short while later for this untimely funeral that was suddenly one of so many. Later, when we were here again, I was sent a little parcel of pale ash and crumbling fragments of bone; we went to the coast and bought two apricot trees and a cherry tree, so as to plant their roots into these fragile remains. The red fruit and the orange fruit would remind me of my almost-daughter's flaming hair.

But still I didn't know what to do with the grief that perched on my shoulder like a bird, holding tight and shifting its weight as I moved. I thought about Adriana who had lost two sons and a husband.

———————————————•———————————————

A few months later I was on the path which goes from our terrace to the cemetery. People here throw bunches of dead flowers haphazardly over the cemetery wall, along with red plastic votive candles, brown plastic flowerpots, leaking metal vases, cellophane wrappers – even tombstones that no longer have a family to claim them. Among all the rubbish I saw a broken piece of marble lying face down. I picked it up and turned it over. There was no name or date on it, just a few floating words written in carefully carved capital letters: . . . *NNE IL TUO RICCORD* . . . *VIVRA NEL NOSTRO CUOR* . . . (YOUR MEMORY SHALL LIVE IN OUR HEARTS).

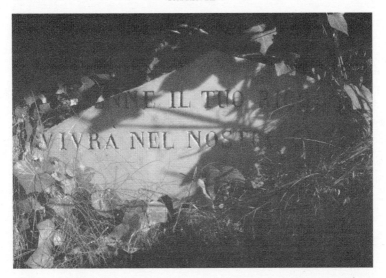

I carried the words home. The stone was heavy and its rough edges bit into the palms of my hands. I found a place to prop it up at the back of the water tank. Reflected in the water, the sunlight flickered on the surface of the marble. The shadow of maidenhair ferns shifted across it and shuddered in the wind. Later, when I had got to know Adriana, I showed her the little memorial and told her its story. '*Brava!*' she said. 'Well done!'

## Patience

But still there was more. In the spring of 2004 Herman's voice changed and he had difficulty swallowing. He went to see a doctor who suspected it might be something serious and we hurried to his home city of Amsterdam so that he could be properly examined.

Solemn specialists in the oncology department gave their verdict and explained their plans. It was too late to operate on the cancer in his throat, so he was to be given a very intense combination of chemotherapy and radiotherapy. Before the treatment started he was fitted with a tube leading directly into his stomach because he would not be able to do any normal eating for several months. He went to be measured for a turquoise-coloured mask to cover his head and shoulders, and to hold him steady on a table while the radiotherapy machine was doing its work. The two of us knew we were preparing for a long siege.

After the second session of chemotherapy, his moustache and the grey curls on one side of his head began to rub off in little clumps on the pillow at night and the accumulating effect of the radiotherapy burnt the skin of his neck and part of his jaw and made his face as swollen as Marco's had been.

We were staying with friends in Amsterdam and they looked after me, while I did my best to look after him, feeding him with packets of liquid food, reading him stories, helping him in any way I could and watching over him as if he were a newborn baby. We laughed and cried very easily. It was a different sort of intimacy from anything we had known before. We were plodding hand in hand along a narrow path with no idea of where it might be leading us.

In order to get a sense of the progress of the treatment I marked the thirty-five radiotherapy sessions and the four chemotherapy sessions on a cloth tape measure and every few days I performed a theatrical ceremony in which I cut off the time that had passed and showed him the shortening length of time that was still to come. I wasn't really sure if it helped him to see me at work with a pair of scissors like one of the Fates, but later he said that it was crucial to witness the past dropping away, while the future became shorter.

As the weeks passed he began to retreat into a very private world. He had lost fourteen kilos, which made his face much more solemn, and his arms and legs were now so thin that you could see the structure of the bones beneath the skin. He hardly spoke, but when he did his voice was small and querulous and seemed to be coming from a great distance. He began to hallucinate. 'I can see the silver thread connecting my soul to my body,' he said one day, sitting hunched up in a wheelchair and looking up into the empty air. 'I don't have to eat food ever again,' he said. 'I only need water. Water is all that matters.'

We were away from the village for eight months. I used to long to be back on our terrace, to see the line of the mountains folding into each other until they reached the Mediterranean; to walk through the garden we had made and sit next to the water tank with its broken words and its celebrating frogs; to see how the new fruit trees were managing and to hear the quarrelling dormice and the swifts cutting through the air like knives.

Finally the treatment was over and the tests were done and the doctors said that as far as they could tell the cancer had gone, although of course in such matters you could never be sure. But for now, at least, there was the chance to go on with the business of living. Herman was still very weak and could hardly find the strength to take more than a few tentative steps, but he was eager to return to the valley. So early in December 2004 we set off and he lay stretched out in the back of the car while I did the driving.

The sky was overcast when we left, but it grew lighter as we moved south. We stayed overnight in the medieval town of Tournus, where we had often stayed before, and in the morning I thought to go to the cathedral, but its big doors were closed so I went to a tourist shop instead and bought a pretty tapestry cushion on which a pale medieval hunting dog with a sharp nose sits in a meadow of little flowers.

By the time we were driving past

the sleeping hulk of Mont Saint Victoire, which Cézanne painted over and over again, the sunshine was briefly with us and that mass of grey rock stood against a backdrop of luminous blue. Then came the turn-off to Marseilles, where we took the motorway running eastwards down the coast, cutting tunnels straight through the mountains and striding over the valleys on concrete legs.

As soon as we crossed the border from France into Italy, the land had that familiar look of cheerful dereliction and instead of prim hotels and villas we were back among clusters of big and shabby greenhouses like those tented refugee encampments that spring up after some disaster. Every so often I would catch sight of a stone house from an earlier time stranded among all the whitened glass, a look of perplexity in its broken windows.

After an hour or so we made the spiralling descent from the motorway back to ground level and took the road that goes up the valley. A new supermarket had erupted out of a plot of waste land and 'Berlusconi = Mussolini' was written in big untidy letters on a concrete wall where before it had said *bimba ti amo* (baby, I love you). We went past the ruins of the Roman fortress, along the narrow main street of the town of the blaspheming ladies, past the rounded outline of the mountain that holds the cave explored by the English lady who was looking for beetles, and past the shrine next to the bridge, where the bus tumbled into the icy water in 1920.

We stopped at Nanda's shop to buy provisions. We went together through the narrow door that released a little cacophony of bells to announce our presence and there were Nanda and her niece Eliana standing side by side behind the counter. Adriana emerged from the little room at the back. All five of us burst into unexpected tears.

'Patience,' said Adriana, looking directly at Herman with her grey eyes. 'We need patience in order to live.'

And to me she said, 'Come and visit me. I am always at home.'

I had a big spiral-bound notebook, which I had been keeping during the months of Herman's illness. It was a way of staying focused while we travelled through such strange and uncharted territory.

On the day after our arrival I wrote:

We reached the house around three o'clock, 6 December. The day was quiet and not cold and when we were standing on the terrace two rainbows appeared in the inward bend of the valley.

The deep water tank is full of tiny goldfish as well as the big blue-ish one that was there when we left. Several frogs in the smaller tank. A toad in the evening light, close to the front door. The rosemary for remembrance has grown huge and determined. The smell of sage and lavender.

On the next day, or perhaps it was the day after that – I didn't make a note of the date – I wrote that our fox terrier had somehow managed to catch a peregrine falcon,

by the tip of its wing, but she released it when I shouted at her. I grabbed her and shut her in the house. The falcon lay in the grass, its wings spread out in a wide mound on either side and it watched me with a yellow eye. I was about to try to pick it up to see if it was wounded, but in my moment of hesitation it lifted into the air and drifted off.

# PART TWO

# WAR AND CHESTNUTS

# Visiting Adriana

Herman was busy with the slow process of recuperation. If the sun was shining he sat in a chair on the terrace and took pleasure in staring towards the triangle of the sea, or he would follow the line of the mountain crests with his eyes. On grey days he would stay inside, reading a bit or moving quietly through the rooms, touching familiar things. He was still fragile and he tired easily, but he was clearly gathering strength and there was a purposefulness and a quiet contentment about him because he had been given this chance of returning to the world.

'Come and see me,' Adriana had said, so I did. I'd go there quite often and talking to her became part of my own process of recuperation after the long months of illness. I'd phone first, to make sure she was not busy, then she would be waiting for me in the courtyard, smiling a welcome, taking me by the hand and leading me through the dark hallway of her house and into the little kitchen where we sat facing each other across a metal table. '*Dimi!*' she'd say and I would ask her questions about the past, and a picture of her life and the life in the village began to take shape. She answered my questions very precisely, pausing to make sure that I understood her, word for word.

I wondered if she would mind if I brought a notebook with me and wrote things down. She said no, not at all, she would like it very much because she didn't want her memories to be lost when she died. So that was how I began. Later I went to talk to other people as well. Little steps.

Adriana said that when she moved to her house there was no road to it, just paths coming in from all directions, so you could choose how you wanted to walk from here to the village by the river, or to the crest of the mountains, or around the bowl of the valley below the treeline.

One path led to the House of the Warm Spring where Old Tunin had lived with his wife La Muta – and it's true that the water from the spring that flows into the big stone tank is much warmer than you would expect. From here you can go through the olive groves to the village of Joseph Sacco the Bandit, who was said to have murdered a priest a long time ago. In an empty house that I believe did belong to Joseph Sacco, I found an eighteenth-century musket lying on the earth floor of a dark room among a confusion of old wine bottles and wooden boxes and a lady's sling-back shoe with a high heel.

If you then took the narrow village street that keeps close to the ridge you would reach the beginning of the Pass of the Man and Woman. It got its name after the two of them fell with their baby, one night when they

were coming home. It took several days to find the bodies and bring them back for burial. The Pass leads to the Cave of the Long Table, but you could only get to it by means of a plank more than three metres in length, which served as a bridge over a sheer drop. This is where the partisans went to hide when they were most in danger, pulling the plank back with them once they had crossed over. Not that they were always safe even then because there were so many informers, people from the village willing to betray them to the Fascists for one reason or another. A man who was known to have been an informer died only two years ago and I was told that some of the old men and women who attended the funeral glanced at each other and bowed their heads in a brief acknowledgement of shared memories.

When the last stretch of the road to the end of the valley was being built in the early 1970s and other little roads were already snaking up and down the steep slopes of the mountains, Adriana's husband and a few of his neighbours realised they had not been included in the plan and so they got hold of a bulldozer and ploughed a narrow zigzag line that would connect all their houses together and allow them to reach the road below. They covered the rough track with a layer of concrete and scratched lines into it while it was still wet, to make a better grip for the tyres.

---

I am on my way to Adriana's house. I drive through a forest of battered chestnut trees, taking the hairpin bends very slowly in case an unseen car is approaching from the other direction. I pass the house belonging to the son of Old Tunin, who is known as Tuninetto or Little Tunin. He is eighty-seven years old, although he doesn't look it. The last time I saw him was at the summer party that is held up on a high pass in the mountains. He had just finished singing some of the partisan songs in a high strong voice, with everyone joining in when they knew the words. He had gone to lie on the meadow grass with a shaggy puppy dog wrapped tightly in his arms and they both had their eyes closed. His house here is painted pink and yellow, and two full-grown hunting dogs on chains bounce up and down when they hear me coming. They emit mournful yodelling cries, their ears flapping like oven gloves.

Little Tunin's olive trees are well pruned so you see the outline of their mottled grey limbs. He also has a number of cherry trees on his terraces and a little shrine, which holds a jam jar of dead flowers and a plastic bottle of holy water from Lourdes, made in the shape of the Virgin Mary with a blue screw-top serving as the crown on her head.

I take a turn to the left and am careful to keep close to the inside wall at the place where Adriana's cousin's truck broke through the fragile edge of the road. Luckily just the two wheels on one side went over, so the truck settled on to its underbelly instead of tumbling down to the terrace below; Adriana's cousin could climb out and everything was all right. Someone has tied pieces of red and white plastic ribbon across the gap, making the scene of potential disaster look quite cheerful and festive.

I park the car where the road comes to an end, get out and walk beside a line of wooden sheds. Three chickens rush forward to welcome me, hurling themselves against the wire mesh of their cage. A solemn duck who is in there with them doesn't share the excitement.

Thin cats sit like sentinels on upturned wooden crates, on piles of squashed cardboard boxes and on the trunk of a tree that has been carved out into a big bowl that once held food for the cow when there was still a cow in the stable. The last one was a black-and-white Friesian and they called her KoeAnna which was the name on the label fixed to her ear when they bought her. They didn't dare to let her out because she was so heavy; the weight of her could easily break through the terrace walls.

The cats stare at me and blink, their bodies tensed in readiness for flight or fight. One has an eye missing.

The walls of the sheds are hung with rusting hooks and chains and mysterious farm implements. A big metal weighing machine with the face of a clock stands in a far corner next to an old tractor covered in sheets of plastic and tied up with rope like a parcel.

Adriana appears at the door. She is wearing a pale yellow cardigan, grey trousers and slippers. Her grey hair is cut short round her head and the sunlight shines through it. Her eyes are deep-set and her features are sharp but very feminine. There is a serenity in her face, yet it flickers with emotion like a little flame. She is much shorter than me and I need to bend forward to kiss her cheek.

She takes hold of my hand. 'How are you?' and she stares at me in order to find out. 'Good,' she says, 'let's get to work.' And she leads me into the house.

We sit in her kitchen. The wood stove is burning. Through the window I can see snow on the crest of the mountains. Lola, the black-and-white hunting dog who no longer hunts, lies under the table and snores. We drink *acquacotta*, water cooked with fruit to make a thin and sweetish gruel. I take out my notebook. 'What do you want to know?' says Adriana. 'Ask me! Ask me about anything and I'll try to answer you.'

I have thought of some of the questions I might ask, but the subject can change course very easily.

'Dormice,' I say. 'What is the dialect name for dormice, and did people eat them? And how do you cook chestnuts? And did you live in this house when you were a child or did you live somewhere else and how old was your father when you were born and when did he die?'

We race along and I scribble down Adriana's answers as fast as I can in my messy handwriting and feel embarrassed when she looks over my shoulder at the words that are looping and tangling across the paper.

Adriana has no preconceptions as to how this all should go and she is unbothered by the way my questions leap from one subject to another. She pauses mid-sentence when she realises she is speaking too fast and sometimes she nods approvingly when she sees me turning a new page. If I don't know a word in Italian and she can't quite explain it to me, I write it phonetically and hope to find it later in the dictionary.

I realise now that by sitting and listening to the story of her life I was trying to pull closer to this place and to my own delicate and tenuous sense of belonging here. And I knew there was something in her way of dealing with fear and sadness that I wanted to learn from.

14 December 2004 (from my notebook):
Today he is less tired than yesterday. He lay in the sun. There is colour

returning to his face. I look at photos from this last year, the hugeness of it all.

28 December
The children have been and gone. Blue days followed by grey days and now a blue and grey day together and all the stoves are lit.

9 January 2005
A cloud of anxiety and sadness sits around me during the day and wakes me into a blank silence during the night. A sense of distance, of loss, of fear, of impatience, of dread. I don't know. I do not know. I am hemmed in, by my self, by the sky and the distant sea.

20 January 2005
And then again, another day and the clouds have shifted. I would like to write about love and old age and travel and the fact of death.

# The Cat-Eating Man

Adriana is telling me about the house by the river where she lived with her family. She says that just like everyone else who was poor, they did the cooking over a fire that was kept burning on the floor of the room where the chestnuts were dried on wire racks close to the ceiling. Chestnuts were hard to prepare and needed to be dried for many weeks with someone feeding the fire through the night as well as the day. Adriana laughs when she remembers approaching the fire on her knees, carrying a pot of soup and closing her eyes while she struggled to suspend it from the hook at the end of its long chain.

Chestnuts made up a huge part of everyone's diet. They would eat them raw, boiled or roasted, drying the nuts on a grille over a fire that was kept burning for around three weeks, day and night. The dried chestnuts would then last into the following year and were especially crucial over the winter. Maybe half the dried nuts were taken to the mill to be ground into flour that could be mixed half and half with wheat flour to make a sort of pasta called *bugaele* or cooked in the oven to make a bread that resembled *focaccia* with olives and salt and a bit of oil. The rest were eaten boiled with milk or water. Adriana says that chestnuts go well with dormice.

There were just two rooms in the house: the chestnut room and the room in which she, her older sister and her parents slept. When she was little they all slept together on sacks filled with dried maize leaves, but then they got two bed frames and mattresses stuffed with the soft branches of briar wood. Until she was fifteen she had only cloth slippers to wear, even in the winter, but when she went to the forest to collect chestnuts or when they all went to hide in the mountains to escape from the Fascists and the German soldiers, she wore an old pair of her father's boots, her feet tiny inside them. She remembers that if you kicked the boots against a stone, the round-headed nails in the soles made little sparks fly, which was like a kind of magic.

Adriana talks about food and how people made a meal out of anything they could find. When she was a child she already knew how to catch eels with a long forked stick and how to trap birds with two stones propped against each other, and how to catch dormice when they were sleeping in the walls of a house or in the hole of a tree. You ate dormouse with potatoes if you had potatoes to eat and they were also good with polenta or boiled chestnuts.

The next time I come to her house she somehow gets on to the subject of mice and how afraid she is of them, and with that she begins the story of *Mangiagatto*, the Cat-Eating Man.

Mangiagatto arrived in the village shortly after the war when so many people were on the move, leaving their homes because of the terrible things they had seen, or because they were hoping for a better way of life somewhere else.

He arrived with nothing, although perhaps he had a sack on his back with nothing much in it. Adriana thought he might have come from the Piedmonte region on the other side of the mountains, but he never said and never explained why he had exchanged one place for another. He rarely spoke to anyone and did not beg for food.

There was an old factory down by the river which had produced cotton thread; many of the women from the village, including her mother, had worked there. But then in the early 1930s it was turned into a military barracks, occupied by Italian troops, and Adriana used to watch them exercising their horses. When the war started the Italians disappeared to fight somewhere far away and the building was empty for a while until German soldiers came and took it over, but they had trucks and lorries rather than horses. It was close to here that there was the big battle by the bridge, the one in which so many men were killed; Adriana had heard the explosions and the gunfire and she had seen the dead bodies, but she didn't want to think about that now, it was too terrible.

The barracks were badly damaged during this battle and some buildings lost their roofs, so when the war was finally over people used the open spaces within the walls to grow vegetables out of the wind or to keep their animals sheltered. But the other rooms, the ones that were more or less intact, were used as living quarters because so much had been destroyed and people were desperate for even the simplest places to live. Adriana and her husband Arturo had taken over one of these rooms when Mangiagatto arrived and he moved in next door.

He had no family, no money and no land, so he had nothing to eat. But he got hold of one of those big demijohn bottles that hold fifty litres of liquid and he cut the top off it with a hot wire so it was more like a big jar. Then he took his sack and went hunting. He hunted for cats, since there were as many stray cats around then as there are now, and he killed them and skinned them and took the meat from their bones and cut it into thin strips and put it in his jar with lots of salt. And that was what he lived on and that was how he got to be called Mangiagatto the Cat-Eater, even though his real name was Beppo.

Adriana says that when she was very pregnant with her first child, a little girl who died within a few days of being born, she was walking past the open door of Mangiagatto's room and he called out to her, 'Come here! Come and look at this!'

He was laughing and holding a big metal frying pan with both hands. Adriana went closer to see what he wanted to show her. His pan was filled with the little bodies of mice; he hadn't even bothered to remove the fur or cut off the thin tails before cooking them.

Adriana screamed and ran away, and she tried to avoid Mangiagatto after that, even though she knew he meant no harm. She says she is sure that is why she is still so frightened of mice and rats because they swoop her back to that time when she was so young and frail and so easily terrified.

# Reptiles

We have two water tanks here, simple concrete basins. I leave a tap dripping to keep the water clear. The frogs are the first to announce the approach of spring. You hear them making a soft purring sound and then when you creep up quietly you might see two or three couples floating together on the surface and singing their song. During the night they produce their cushions of spawn and during the day you might catch sight of them, proudly resting their frog arms on the myriad black dots of life.

The toads come later, just a single pair, a large female and her diminutive partner. They blink and gulp under the shelter of the water-lily leaves and sing no songs. I have never seen their spawn even though I have occasionally seen a tiny toad making the difficult journey from one place to another. And once I saw a salamander perched on the side of the tank, but I never spotted it again.

It's these slow reptiles that I like best, the ones that pretend to be a stone as you watch them, so you can observe the flickering of an eyelid over a golden eye, the pulsating heartbeat in the throat, the splayed fingers, the stretched-back legs with their curiously human thighs. But I can spend ages watching tadpoles: their hopefulness and their helplessness as they go through the process of metamorphosis from one sort of creature into another.

# Half-People

When Adriana says how hungry she was as a child and as a young woman, it doesn't make sense to me. During the war, of course, when the men were fighting somewhere far away or later when they had come back and were hiding like foxes in the forests and mountain caves, but surely not before the war started, or later once it was over?

'You had goats and rabbits,' I say. 'You grew vegetables and planted little fields of wheat and collected the chestnuts, you caught thrushes and eels and dormice . . .'

'We were *mezzadri*,' she replies, interrupting me. When I still don't understand, she crosses one index finger over the other, to divide it in half.

Almost everyone in the village were *mezzadri* or half-people, which meant that they owned nothing for themselves. They belonged to a *padrone* who was their master and they had to give him half of everything they produced, down to the last kilo of olives or chestnuts, the last egg or cabbage. One old man told me how his father took a cartload of plums to the *padrone*'s grand house a few miles away, pulling the load himself because he had no mule. The *padrone* inspected this offering, said the quality was not good enough, then tipped the fruit on to the ground and laughed. Another *padrone* from round here demanded his share of the women as well, but that is another story.

If you were sick and couldn't work, or when the harvest failed because of heavy rains or a frost, you still had to supply the usual weight of produce, even though the mathematics of such a division might leave you with almost nothing for yourself. During the war it fell to the women, children and old people to fill the quota. When the German soldiers came to the valley in 1944 they went from house to house taking anything they could find, while the *padrone* expected supplies of food to be brought to the military bases and never mind if you were helping to feed the same soldiers who had killed your son or your brother, or had burnt your house to the ground.

The three wealthy *padroni* who had control over this part of the valley were very strict in their demands. They all employed land agents who lived in the villages and knew exactly what was being produced and where. These agents were there at each stage of the year with their weighing machines and notebooks and pencils, ready to divide the spoils.

'There was the Engineer,' says Adriana. 'He was here most of the time, living in the big house you can see from my window. He never married, but still everyone knew he had children – two sons and maybe there were others as well.'

Then there was the Marquis from Rome who owned the patch of chestnut forest where Adriana's family worked, but he was always away in the city and nobody knew anything about him, although Adriana says she saw him once much later when he was visiting the Engineer. He was an old man wearing a hat and a silk cravat. He stared blankly at her, but he didn't say anything and she kept silent.

Adriana says she can't have been more than five years old when her father explained what it meant to be half-people. She had asked him why he always gave their food away, even though they had so little for themselves. 'We are nothing and we own nothing,' he told her. 'We don't own the walls of the houses we have built, or the land that we work on.' She remembered that he was upset by his own words and she tried to argue with him, saying she was not half a person and he must have made a mistake – and that made him angry, even though he was a man who rarely showed anger.

Her father hardly ever spoke when he was at home, but he talked a lot to Adriana when they were working together in the forest. They would sit side by side with a bit of bread and perhaps some cheese in the middle of the day and he would tell her all sorts of things. 'He was very precise in his use of words,' she says.

He was a cold man, her father, and he never once hugged her or gave her a kiss or invited her to sit on his lap, but she knew he had a good heart and she was satisfied with her friendship with him.

For her part she tried to be like a son for him. He was not interested in hunting wild animals because he didn't like to use a gun, but he taught her how to set traps for small birds and how to catch eels. They always took the goats with them when they went out and she helped him clear the ground in the chestnut forest. When he cut firewood, which he could then sell, she piled it up. Another of her jobs was watering the crops planted on the terraces, opening and closing the network of ditches that led from the big water tank.

He often spoke about the things that had happened to him before he married and had a family. He had been a soldier in the other war, the one he called the 1918, and the cold and the hunger were worse than anything he had known since. Once he was in the mountainous Veneto region with a bayonet but no bullets, and he and his comrades were caught in an ambush. When the shooting was over he crawled out from under a heap of dead men who had been his friends.

He lived in France for several years after that; 'until I stopped shaking,'

he said. While he was there he fell in love with a young Frenchwoman and wanted to marry her, but he left her and came back to the village because he had been promised to Adriana's mother and she was waiting for him.

And in the spring of 1940, when Adriana was just six years old and a new war was drawing closer month by month, her father said he was sure it was going to be much worse than that last one, because it was turning into a war between the people of Italy and that meant that no one would know who were their friends and who were their enemies. Even families would turn against each other, he said.

---

'Enough!' and she gets abruptly to her feet and washes her hands in the sink. She asks if I would like to see her collection of stones. She opens the glass door that leads to the covered terrace and we step out into the shaded sunshine. Lola the dog comes too, with soft shuffling steps.

The terrace is filled with stones. There are heaps of them on the floor and on a table next to an electric iron and a plastic bucket filled with food for the chickens. There are stones on chairs, on the water tank, on an old washing machine. They are all shapes and sizes; some would fit easily into a pocket and others would be hard to lift; some are limestone that appears as smooth and elastic as chewing gum and others are honeycomb lumps of *tufa* that have grown into being out of the slow dripping of water; there are stones that look like strange monsters, pieces of slate bearing the delicate

imprint of fossilised ferns and lumps of quartz and glittering quartz crystals. Adriana says she has collected stones all her life and her husband used to find them for her in the mountains. Sometimes he would come back carrying a stone on his head in the way that women used to carry water or big baskets of goods. He presented them to her as if they were expensive gifts from a fine shop.

She says that when she looks at her stones they bring her closer to an understanding of God and they make her feel quiet on days when she does not feel quiet. When she dies she wants her children to heap the stones on her grave, instead of flowers. She has told them so and she hopes they will agree to do it and that the priest won't object.

# Stones

I said, 'I collect stones too, and fossils,' and as I said it I could see myself many years ago, living in a little house in Suffolk. Every morning after my children had gone to school I'd set out on a very determined walk with my shaggy biscuit-coloured dog to keep me company. I'd head for a particular field: a wide, blank expanse of heavy ploughed clay in the winter and wheat in the summer, and I'd move across it in a kind of trance of concentration, searching for fossils and for unbroken flints with a shape that pleased me.

There was a little dip in the field that was always the most productive, so that I imagined some ancient sea swirling and eddying over this one point and dumping its miscellaneous treasures just here. I found dozens of the mussel-like shells known as Devil's Toenails, because they do look as if they have been plucked from the toes of some ancient and almost human creature. I found the perfectly rounded heads of ammonites pinpricked with lines of little holes from which their sharp spikes had once sprouted, and a white fan-shaped scallop complete with the fossilised sand, which had settled between its two open halves. There was one that appeared to be the root of a water-lily and another that looked like the first metamorphosis of life: an explosion of energy stretching its petrified tentacles across a smooth lozenge of stone. And every so often I would find a flint as smooth as jelly and moulded into the shape of the torso of a thin man, or the luxuriant body of a reclining woman, or some other unexpected image.

The dog watched me and grew bored while I scavenged and after a while we'd return home. I'd lay out my stones on tables and window ledges so I could admire them and read the stories they seemed to tell me. And somewhere within that whole process I would find the sort of quiet inside myself that Adriana calls patience. And just like her I sometimes thought that when I died I would like to have my grave covered with a thick heap of the stones I had found.

In Suffolk I also used to go and talk to elderly men and women about the old days, and I wrote down little snippets of what they told me. There was a man called Kenny. I suppose he was in his eighties by the time I got to know him. Two of his children, the two boys, had both been born simpletons and even though they lived a number of years and became the size of full-grown men, they never learnt to talk or walk.

Kenny led me through the garden where he would bring his boys to lie out in the sunshine and he showed me the wooden skateboard constructions he made, so they could manage a sort of paddling movement along the paths. In one of the flowerbeds he had placed a big hag-stone flint with a hole through its centre; it looked far too heavy to roll to one side, let alone to lift. Kenny said he had found it in a field over on the other side of the low hill behind his house and he had carried it home on his back, even though the weight had almost crippled him. He said he didn't know why he had done that, except that he wanted to have the stone close to him.

And now Adriana shows me stones that her husband brought to her that are just as heavy as that flint. He would find them when he was out hunting in the high mountains and in spite of his limp, which made walking so much more difficult, he would carry them home so she could put them with the others on the terrace; stare at them and wonder at their ancient strangeness and the stories they seemed to tell.

# Writing Things Down

Another day and we are back in the kitchen. The mountains look dark against the brilliant blue of the sky. We drink strong coffee in little cups and Adriana has made a cake with flour and sugar and olive oil and pieces of apple.

Adriana says that she enjoys telling me all these things about the past.

She says that since she has started talking to me like this her memories have become much more alive. She can look back at the happy times with the people she loved and she can even allow herself to look at the sad times and at the memories that she has tried to hide because they have frightened her so much.

A few years ago, when her husband and her eldest son had both died in such quick succession, she thought she was losing her mind. She was trapped in a mist of despair and she hardly knew where she was or who she was any more. She could make no plans and would even forget what she had done on the previous day or a few minutes before.

She wanted to escape, from her house, from the village, from the valley. She had no idea where she might go, but she thought if she could get to the railway station she would catch the first train that came in and see where it took her.

She put her purse in her pocket, packed a few clothes in a bag and started walking down the concrete road that her husband and his friends had made, but she hadn't got far when her cousin drove past in his truck and he stopped and talked to her and took her home again.

'I realised then that I couldn't leave. I have my daughters here and my grandchildren. So that was when I began to write things down in a note-book like the one you use,' she says, staring at me to make sure I am following her. 'I wrote everything that came into my mind: stories from my childhood, events that happened last week, or last month: a baptism, the fact that the grapes were ready to be harvested, the rabbits having babies. I wrote about my marriage and my life with Arturo and about my children who are living and how much I love them and about the ones I have lost and how much I miss them. Putting the words down gave me patience. It made it possible for me to survive.'

Adriana has kept the notebook in a box and she adds to it sometimes, but she doesn't reread it. She says she won't ever show it to anyone, but after her death her children and grandchildren can find it and maybe then they will know her better. She hopes they will ignore the spelling mistakes and the untidy writing.

'There are many things that I haven't the strength to tell them. I have

76

never been able to put words to my inner thoughts, the thoughts that lie in my head, because I never studied like you have,' she says. 'I stopped going to school when I was eleven and before then it was sometimes difficult to go because of the war. I wish it had been possible for me to learn more. But my teacher was pleased with me and said I was a good pupil. I can still remember some of the poems of Manzoni that they taught me and I enjoyed writing the stories we were told to write about ourselves. We also studied history: Napoleon mostly and the books talked a lot about Mussolini. There were photographs of him surrounded by schoolchildren in the black-and-white Fascist uniform, which I had to wear as well. My father hated Mussolini and the whole idea of Fascism, but what could he do, he was too old to fight.'

Adriana has hardly been away from this valley. 'But when I was fourteen I was given the chance to go away for ever,' she says and she tells me how she was by the river with her goats when she met a very grand Englishwoman who arrived out of nowhere in a big black car and started talking to her and offered to take her to England as her travelling companion. She says she often thinks about that meeting and the way that a new path of destiny had suddenly opened up before her; if she had gone along that path, who knows what direction her life might have followed. She says she has photographs of the Englishwoman somewhere and she will look for them and try to remember her name. Later she will tell me more of the story.

She returns to thoughts of leaving the valley. Once, long ago when she was only recently married, she and her husband and a couple of his friends took a train and then a bus until they had reached the mountains further down the coast. They slept on hay in a barn and they hunted marmot and hare, and then they came home again. They were gone for five days. She has also visited a relative who was living in the Piedmonte region close to the Swiss border, but she didn't stay long. She and her husband went by bus to Lourdes to pray for a miracle when her son was first told that he had cancer. She thinks maybe that helped because the illness went away for a while, but then it came back.

5 February 2005 (from my notebook):
The sky has turned grey after so many weeks of intense blueness in the soft winter sun. Yesterday we did a walk with Eliana and Massimo, up high, surrounded by mountains, a vision of eternity. A flock – or is it a herd or a gathering – of chamois, perhaps forty or more, shifting like shadows across a steep slope. Banks of snow carved into strange shapes by the wind on the crest of the Pass of the Garland. Five hours of walking and his face has taken some colour from the sun and no longer looks so swollen.

19 February 2005
Snow falls but melts on the ground and the air is still and silent and the moon is muzzy behind a thin film of cloud, and on 5 April it will be six years since I first set foot in this house, my heart to his heart.

# With Eliana

I got to know Adriana's daughter Eliana when she invited me to come with her to a weekly keep-fit class on the coast. This must have been six years ago, before we had met her brother Marco and his dogs, before Herman's accident in the car and before all the other events that tumbled around us like a landslide sweeping down from the mountainside, carrying away trees and paths and all the solid ground you were used to standing on.

We'd set off in Eliana's car which until her pregnancy and the birth of her son, she drove with a cheerful recklessness. As she sped round tight corners, hooting her horn more as a greeting than a warning, we would be talking so much and so intensely that I forgot I was using a foreign language.

Eliana sparkles and when she is particularly happy she seems to purr like a cat. She shares her mother's clarity of speech and they also both have a quality of directness that makes it possible to talk about anything. On our trips to the coast we described the lives we have lived so far and the people we have known. I told her about my bohemian parents in London and she told me about her childhood here in the valley. And when my friend died and her brother's illness returned, we still went to the gym whenever we could and we went on talking.

In the changing room Eliana introduced me as her friend who was living here in the valley. She acted as an interpreter if I failed to understand the babble of questions that were asked of me.

We were mostly female gymnasts, although there was one slightly downtrodden husband accompanying his very raucous wife who liked to make rude jokes and then went red in the face from laughing at them. There was also an octogenarian with spindly legs who spent a lot of time sitting on a bench watching the action and a solemn young man with learning difficulties who could get fascinated by the strangeness of his own reflection. He would go and stand right in front of the mirror that faced us all, staring at himself with a bemused smile on his face. 'You are beautiful! You are beautiful and we love you, come back to us!' several of the women would then cry to him in loud voices, until the spell was broken and he returned to his place in the line and class continued. We always began on the exercise bicycles, shifting the settings so that we were struggling up steep slopes, before racing downhill so fast it was hard to keep your feet on the pedals.

Our instructor was a lean little man who bounced on his toes and treated us like a herd of unruly cattle, slapping one lady on her flank when she was not pedalling hard enough and telling us to think about our husbands when we lay on our backs squeezing big soft rubber balls between our knees, to the accompaniment of loud disco music. I told Eliana that in England he'd never get away with such talk, but she just said he was a good man with a good heart.

It was Eliana who first took me to the Hermit's Cave, not long after we were back from Amsterdam. She thought she could find the way, even though it might have changed a lot since the last time she was there. At the start of the path some men were busy pruning the olive trees and burning the thin branches. They called out to us, asking where we were going.

'To the Hermit,' Eliana called back and they replied by shaking a loose hand and making a guttural 'eough! eough!' sound, which meant that it wouldn't be easy to do.

The terrace walls were made of stones as big as cartwheels, balanced in a careful mosaic. There were all sorts of unexpected flowers along the path – clumps of madonna lilies and angelica and asphodel – and Eliana said that the women used to plant flowers, to make the way more pleasing. We passed a big prickly pear with a few initials cut into the fat slab of one of the leaves. Eliana said the old woman called Rinuccia had cut those letters long ago, so we were not lost.

We came to a little hut and then we were on the terraces that belonged to Eliana's family, from her mother's side, and she thought the hut was the one where her grandfather used to leave food for the Hermit, but she wasn't sure.

The path vanished and Eliana went searching for it, darting about like a dog looking for rabbits, with me following rather more ponderously behind and both of us laughing at the steepness of it all and at the strange magic that can make you confident of where you are in one moment and utterly lost in the next.

By now we had left the olive trees behind and everything was very precarious. If you slipped and fell you would hurtle down to the road far below. Eliana told me how her aunt fell from a wall when she was very little; she landed safely and no bones were broken and when people asked her what had happened she said her father was there and he caught her in his arms and smiled as he held her and set her gently on the ground. But her father had died a few weeks before in an accident while he was bringing wood down from the mountains and so everyone believed that a miracle had occurred.

We clambered up over some rocks and threaded our way forward through thorny bushes, but that only brought us out to the edge of a ravine from where we had a good view of the bandit Joseph Sacco's village and the Pass of the Man and Woman. Once again Eliana disappeared ahead of me and this time she let out a cry of triumph.

Here we were on a platform of rock that was like a little garden with a low wall built around it and a bush with pink lavatera flowers which I have never seen anywhere else in the wild, looking as if it had been planted by a careful gardener. The entrance to the cave was in front of us. We needed to bend our heads to go inside and it was like a room, the earth floor clean and dry. There was a sort of bench at the far end, a stone platform that would serve as a bed and a round hole further up in the rock wall like a window.

'I'll show you the paintings he made,' said Eliana. She led me up to a narrow ledge of rock that was part of the roof of the cave. The wax-smooth wall of coloured limestone behind it was covered in writing and images.

We had disturbed a big bird of prey and it suddenly fell out into the sky from somewhere close by our heads. We watched its silhouette sweeping out into the wide channel of air and growing smaller and smaller until it had vanished. I wondered if the Hermit was ever tempted to surrender himself to such a trusting leap into space and out of time.

We sat in the sunshine and ate bread and cheese, and I suppose it was the isolation of the place and the story of the man who had made it his home that brought us to talk about the fact of death and how incomprehensible it is that someone lives and then dies. Eliana said she sometimes felt people staring at her because they could see the tragedies that have surrounded her and it made her afraid; it made her feel as if her destiny was somehow tainted and everyone she loved might die. She asked me about my almost-daughter with the red hair and I said she was someone who loved rock climbing and parachuting and anything that brought her closer to a particular sense of freedom, and then it was as if that familiar presence was sitting with us, looking out across the valley.

We went further along the platform and round a corner, and there was a wooden beehive carefully positioned in a sheltered corner with a flat stone on its little roof, presumably to keep it steady in a storm. The planks of dark chestnut wood were cracked and dry, but still strong.

'It might have belonged to the Hermit,' said Eliana, 'or perhaps the partisans carried it here. Who can tell?'

# Scooter Woman

I sometimes think that I have never learnt anything new in all my life. I began writing because I liked to write things down. I learnt foreign languages because they seemed to enter my head by a process of osmosis. When I was young I danced alongside everyone else in a sort of enthusiastic wiggle in response to the beat of the music, but I never learnt any steps and now I feel foolish because I do not know how to do the foxtrot or the samba.

But then in 2003, before all our troubles, Herman bought a scooter. He said it made much more sense to do short journeys on a scooter rather than in a car, and on top of that there was the wind in your face, the lightness of movement, the simplicity of it all.

For months I stared balefully at this new machine. I would sit behind Herman on the passenger seat, grasp him round the middle and try not to be too stiff when turning sharp corners, but I refused to try to drive it. Then one day I turned the key in the ignition, revved the accelerator on the handlebar and, like a bird learning to fly, launched myself forward into this unfamiliar element and did not fall into a ditch or collide with a tree.

As I was coming up the road from the shop, there were old Armando and his wife repairing a pothole since no one else was going to do it. They heard my put-puttering approach, stopped in their work and looked up. I was approaching so slowly and obviously, with such a look of nervous trepidation on my face, that they began to roar with laughter. Armando made a turning gesture with his hand in appreciation of my slowness and I tried to smile, which meant that I briefly lost concentration and almost fell off. But I got home. And later, when I was more at ease on such a vulnerable machine, I could wave with one hand to the people I was passing and they would wave back and I felt triumphant in a tiny sort of way.

Scooter Woman, Herman called me, and later, when we came here after the treatment and he was so exhausted and enfeebled that he hadn't the strength to drive it, I took him on little expeditions, setting off with complete confidence, feeling his arms round me and the extra weight of his body as I negotiated the curves. I thought of those scooter journeys when Armando told me how the women would carry their swaddled babies in a basket balanced on their heads when they were walking the steep paths and of course they never slipped and fell.

# The Hermit's Story

Adriana told me more about the Hermit. She said he shared the same surname as her father and they were either cousins or second cousins, she wasn't sure, but certainly they both came from the village higher up from here, closer to the summit of the mountain. 'Maybe you can drive me there one day,' she said. 'I like to take flowers to my mother and father in the cemetery and now that Arturo has gone it's not so easy.'

Adriana's father was one of eleven children and seven of them stayed on in that village. As a child she would visit them when she could, following the mule track that went up from the river, built like a staircase in cobbled stones. There was an uncle who helped build the track and an uncle who could make leather shoes and another uncle who mended old umbrellas. He was the one who knew how to repair watches and clocks as well, even though no one had ever taught him. He was called Giobatta of the Arches because his house was in the centre of the village where there were arches on all sides and he had a grey beard like a spade that grew down to his waist. The children would scream when they saw him, so he kept little apples in his pocket, which he offered to them to make them less afraid. It was this uncle who made the engraved drawings in the slate bench under an arch by the stone drinking trough close to his house; the slab of black stone is covered with cartoon-like images of cats and clocks and church steeples, as well as a man with a big beard and a roaring lion with a crown on its head.

The Hermit was born in 1876. Everyone knew that because he had cut the date of his birth into the rock above his cave, alongside his own name and the names of his mother and father, his brothers and sisters; the words heaped up on top of each other in an elegant little tower.

There was apparently nothing wrong with the Hermit when he was a young man, although perhaps he was shy, as people can be when they see very few strangers in the early years of their life. Just like one of Adriana's uncles, he was skilled at making the cobbled surfaces of paths and roads. He was out with a group of men mending a lower part of the road that followed the river towards the coast, when there was a *frana* or landslide and heavy stones fell down and hit him in the face, smashing through his eyebrows, his nose and his jaw. It looked terrible and everyone who was with him thought he would surely die.

They made a stretcher and carried him back to his home in the high village. There was nothing to be done; even Pietro the bonesetter, who knew how to mend broken legs and arms by forcing them back into position with one quick movement and then binding them up – even he could not repair such intricate damage. The Hermit lay in bed with a high fever for a long time while his parents watched over him.

Gradually he recovered and eventually he was able to eat and to walk again. But when he felt the changed shape of his face and saw his own reflection, he panicked and ran from his home. He followed the same path that Eliana and I had followed until he reached the cave that everyone knew about, because it was so perfectly shaped, so well protected. And there he remained for many years.

People from the village knew where he was but they didn't try to bring him back. They pitied him and understood that he didn't want to be seen, so they brought food for him and other things that might be useful: blankets, a little oil lamp. They left these offerings in an abandoned hut below the cave. Adriana's father remembered having to go there as a child carrying food for the Hermit and being afraid that he might be confronted by the man with the terrible face, but he never once saw him.

When the weather was cold, the Hermit lit a fire in the front of his cave and the people could see the thin thread of smoke. He collected chestnuts, which he could roast over the fire, and made himself a bed from the soft branches of the boxwood bushes that grew close by. He built a dry-stone wall in the mouth of the cave to make it less exposed, and another wall to enclose a patch of soil like a little garden. One winter somebody might have brought him a beehive filled with sleeping bees and he set that up on the narrow ledge and collected the honey they made.

So there he was, near his own village and yet as far away as someone who had died long ago. People who passed beneath the cave sometimes heard him praying or singing in a loud voice, but nobody went to see him for fear that he might be afraid. Then one day he no longer collected the food that was left out for him, so they knew he must have died. They went to fetch

his body, to bring it back to the little cemetery in the village.

That was when they saw for the first time that the cliff face above the cave was decorated with carvings. The Hermit must have used a knife to cut words and pictures into the rock. He had beautiful calligraphy and could write Latin as well as Italian. He made a drawing of a sailing ship carrying two angels and above it he wrote in Latin, 'Heaven on Earth for all Eternity'. He made a drawing of three crosses on a hill and next to it he made a face surrounded by what looks like a crown of thorns and the figure in profile of a man on his knees with his hands raised in prayer and the words 'Ave Maria'.

The cave, its little garden and the platform of rock above it became a sort of shrine. It was known as the Balcony of Ecstasy and people said that some of the drawings were done in blood and the blood was never washed away by the rain from one year to the next, and that in itself was a sort of miracle.

# Cemeteries

That time of illness changed us. I had become less afraid of the uncertain future and each new day felt like a bonus.

We had conversations, he and I, about how I would manage if he should die. He said I had made my home here in the valley and people would watch over me if I was on my own; our children would come and visit me and friends too. He said laughingly that I could write a book in which a recently widowed Englishwoman drives to her home in the Italian mountains with her husband's ashes in the back of the car. I was glad to look such thoughts in the face.

We wrote our wills, Italian wills, which means you write it in ink in your very best handwriting on a sheet of paper and you can't make a copy because that is not valid. Then you place the will in a cupboard or a drawer where it can be found later, although goodness knows what happens if the house burns down and takes your will with it. There was a sense of clarity making the simple divisions of property, writing out each other's names and the names of our three children who will follow on from us.

And in that same mood of calm practicality we went to the local town council and asked about booking a burial plot, because it suddenly seemed like a nice idea to have a place in the little cemetery that we pass so often when we are setting off for a walk in the mountains. We were told that there was a waiting list for the marble boxes like big chests of drawers in which one's bones can be laid, but there was no such problem and nothing to pay if we simply wanted to be interred in a hole in the ground. We said we would like a double plot, a matrimonial bed as it were, and the man behind the office desk grinned and said he would make a note of it.

So now, when we go past the walled cemetery with its families of Stones and Cockerels, the two young men who were shot in February 1944, the very old man who seems to have been buried with his mule and all the others who lie there, I wonder whether we will join them one day with our foreign surnames and perhaps even with a portrait photograph printed on to a china disc just like everyone else has. Then our children can come and visit us and can remember us when they look at a little photograph of our faces.

# The Patchwork Woman

Back in Adriana's kitchen on another day and there is the sound of a car drawing up and hooting its horn. 'It's the postman,' says Adriana. 'He comes here even when he has no letters for me because he likes to drink wine.'

She goes to open the door and it squeaks over the tiles on the floor. The postman enters carrying a limp advertising leaflet in his hand, which he presents to Adriana with a slightly apologetic flourish. She nods to a chair and he sits down obediently. He is thin and hollow-cheeked and looks as exhausted as the leaflet that now lies on the table.

'Wine?' says Adriana, filling a tumbler before he has answered.

The postman drinks two glasses of Adriana's pale yellow wine in quick succession, then he clearly feels better. He says the weather is warm and the wine is good and he sighs and smiles and thanks Adriana and shakes my hand.

'Until tomorrow!' she calls after him as he leaves.

Rinuccia arrives a few moments later. She lives further up the hill in the big house that belonged to the *padrone* they called the Engineer. It still belongs to the *padrone*'s descendants.

Rinuccia is on her way back from the bus that dropped her off at the bottom of the road – like so many of the older women here, she never learnt to drive a car. She calls out as she pushes open the heavy front door, then she enters the kitchen and gives me and the sleeping dog a brief greeting and says something very fast to Adriana in dialect. She refuses the offer of wine. She sits down with a grunting sigh, on the chair vacated by the postman.

Rinuccia is eighty-two years old but she appears very strong and upright and somehow spiky. She is wearing thin walking shoes, rolled-down ankle socks, a narrow skirt that comes just below the knee and a grey cardigan with a ball of string bulging in one pocket, with what looks like a very ancient and well-tailored man's waistcoat on top of it all.

I know from Adriana that the Engineer had no wife, but he made use of any of the women or young girls that he wanted, just a sign or a word of command and they had to go to meet him in a stone building behind the vineyards and there was no chance of disobedience because then your whole family would be punished. Everyone said the *padrone* was the father of two sons and one of them was chosen as heir to his land, his property and his power in the village, while the other, whose name was Tunin, remained a *mezzadro*.

The son who had been chosen as the new *padrone* was sent away to study at a university and then he was given a fine villa on the coast. He married, but his wife died shortly after giving birth to a boy and that was when Rinuccia was summoned. She moved to the coast to live with him as his housekeeper and she looked after his baby as if it were her own. As time went by she also looked after her master as if she were his wife, even though she remained his servant. When he grew old, the *padrone* and Rinuccia returned to the big house in the village and she cared for him right to the end, even when he had forgotten his own name or how to dress or eat with a spoon. I wonder if it is his waistcoat that she is now wearing.

Rinuccia's grey hair is straight and cut into a shaggy crop held in place with hairgrips, which must be what gives her such a girlish look in spite of her age. The skin of her face is much darker and more weatherbeaten than Adriana's and covered with a mass of symmetrical lines that look as formal as tribal scars, but in a photograph of her as a young girl you can see how beautiful she was, with high Slavic cheekbones, almond-shaped almost lidless eyes, a wide mouth and big flat teeth.

Adriana has told me that Rinuccia's father had long side whiskers, which made him look very fierce and everyone was frightened of him. Her elder

brother and her fiancé were sent to fight on the Russian front, and they both disappeared and never returned. When the war came to the valley, she and one of her two sisters joined the partisans up in the mountains, just the two of them in the company of twelve men. That was how she knew all the paths so well and learnt how to curse.

After the death of the man who had been both her master and her husband, and after the child who had been like a son to her had moved away to live on the coast, Rinuccia stayed on alone in the big house. She has no dogs or cats to keep her company and if she is not working on the land, she is out walking in the forest and up to the top of the mountains. She searches for mushrooms when they are in season or else she just walks for the pleasure of it. Quite recently she went as far as the Hermit's Balcony of Ecstasy and announced that the blood of his paintings was fading; a couple of years ago she told Eliana that she had been to the Pass of the Man and Woman, even though it's so steep and narrow that few people would dare to go that way.

Adriana explains to Rinuccia that I want to know stories about the village in the old days and the conversation quickly turns to Benedetta the beggar woman who used to live close by. Rinuccia tells me with a snort that the name means a blessing.

'I was on the terraces with my friends,' she says. 'Benedetta was sitting with her back to the wall, saying her prayers as she always did. We stood in a line above her and we pissed on her head. She thought it was a miracle. She said, "Oh, what warm rain is falling on me!"'

With that Rinuccia gets to her feet and holds her hands up like the Virgin Mary at the Annunciation, saying again, '"Oh, what warm rain!"' while looking at the ceiling to see where it might have come from.

Adriana laughs a bit shyly and says she only saw Benedetta once when she came to their door begging for food, but she remembers hearing her singing and praying as she approached and she remembers the strange clothes she wore. She made long, loose dresses for herself from pieces of old sacking, which she sewed together with the thin branches of broom that people still use to tie up the vines after pruning.

'She used bits of wire as well, for the stitching, and she smelt – Mother of God how she smelt!' says Rinuccia. 'She never cooked her food, she ate everything raw, even meat or chestnuts she ate raw. I looked into the kitchen, which was the only room she used in her house, and there was a long table covered with flies. Black with flies and the noise of them!' and Rinuccia makes the 'eough!' sound to explain just how terrible the noise was and even more terrible the smell.

'Benedetta had no bed in that room,' she continues. 'She slept in a chair with her head on the table. Some hunters came by and opened the door and saw her sleeping, and they shot through the leg of the chair as a joke and she fell to the floor. But she didn't get the joke because she didn't understand such things.

'She walked all day, going from house to house even in the rain, begging for food. You would hear her coming because of the prayers. She never went inside; she stood at the door and people put food in her hands. She could walk through the dark of the night as well, like a cat. She had many cats and they would follow in a line behind her.'

I ask about Benedetta's family and Adriana says she came from the same high village where her own father was born. 'She went away from there and she never wanted to return. I don't know why she was always on her own.'

'It was because the man called Giovanetto found her walking on the road one night,' says Rinuccia. 'It was after that she came to live in the house here. She kept saying, "He made a hole in me with his pee-pee!" But people only laughed at her.'

And with that Rinuccia blows her nose on a big man's handkerchief and gets ready to leave. She shakes my hand and gives me a little military nod before she goes.

'She makes me angry and she keeps me company,' says Adriana when her neighbour has gone. And then in the sunshine we walk very slowly to the house among the chestnut trees where Benedetta used to live.

The house is built of pale yellow stones. Its roof went long ago and the skeleton of the building is slowly disintegrating. A rusty white enamel chamber pot hangs from a hook on an outside wall and a clump of blue

amaryllis are growing wild close to what was once the front door. I look at what was once the doorway and try to imagine Benedetta emerging from her dark room, the flies buzzing, the smell of her, the sound of her singing.

# The Bat and the Snake

Just a few days ago I went to get my slippers from the bedroom, where they were placed side by side under the window. When I stooped to pick up the slippers I saw a large bat next to them on the floor. It shuffled about a bit with its wings and I noticed it had a short but rather mouse-like tail, which meant it was a species known as the European Free-Tailed Bat, its colour, according to my guidebook, 'uniformly drab' and its habits 'little known'.

I opened the window as a first step towards doing something practical, but as I did so, a snake fell down and landed in a wriggling heap on the window ledge. The bat had meanwhile partially hidden itself under a suitcase. The snake, after a bit more thrashing, climbed up the side of the window and managed to knot its tail into what looked like a second hinge while holding the rest of its body vertically in line with the window frame. I looked at it and saw the glint of its eye as it looked back at me, but it kept perfectly still.

I went to get some leather gloves and with the help of my daughter, I lifted the suitcase. I picked up the bat, which opened its mouth wide and made high-pitched and threatening squeaks, showing a moist pink tongue and very sharp teeth. I released the bat in the woodshed and when I came back to see what the snake was doing it had disappeared. I think it must have been a young Rat Snake, which people here call a *rateia*. I once saw a big one standing – as it were – on the tip of its tail, holding itself vertical and swaying slightly. It managed to find a little branch to twist round and then the entire body followed, hauled up like a length of rope.

# The House of the Stair

It was Rinuccia who took me to see the room where Old Tunin was born. 'Come, I'll show you!' she said, striding ahead of me, wearing the same clothes she always wears, but with an apron on top and a little bunch of fresh broom twigs sticking out of the pocket for binding up the grapevines.

The House of the Stair stands on the edge of the vine terraces above the *padrone*'s house and gazes out like a sentinel across the valley. It's a tiny building and it got its name from the delicate arch of stone steps on the external wall that leads to the upper room.

Rinuccia climbs the steps as quick as a goat. She moves the piece of wood tied to a length of rope that serves as a lock for the door and pushes the door open. She tells me to hurry up and follow her.

The room we enter is roughly twelve feet long and eight feet wide with a single shuttered window and a little triangular fireplace in one corner and a tiny triangular sink carved from a piece of slate in the other. The sink is not connected to a tap, but it does have a hole through which water can drain down the outside wall of the building. Renuccia is very proud of this detail, 'No one else had something like this,' she says, stroking the grey stone.

Old Tunin and his elder brother were born in this room and the whole family lived here and worked on the *padrone*'s land that surrounded them, although they spent some time up in the high pastures during the summer and in a hut in the forest during the chestnut harvesting season.

The room is empty of furniture. I suppose it might have held a table and a couple of benches, but there is certainly no space for beds, so everyone must have slept together on hay spread out across the floor. When I suggest rather tentatively that it's not a very big place for so many people, Rinuccia gives me a disdainful look and says there were many much smaller houses in which ten people were crammed together. 'At least they kept warm!' she says with one of her little snorts. 'But the slate roof was always leaking and they had no blankets to cover themselves with so when it rained they filled wide cane baskets with chestnut leaves and slept under them, and that provided a bit of shelter. The grandparents had the room below,' she says, 'and it is not as big as this one and has no window. The door is locked so I can't show you.'

We go to look at the barn built on to the side of the House of the Stair. Its thick door has a crack right across the upper section, where the dark wood is marked with a series of curious half-moon indentations. 'The Fascists, looking for partisans! They hit it with the butts of their rifles but the door did not break! It was too strong for them,' says Rinuccia as she pounds her fist triumphantly against the wood.

'Now, read this!' and she points her finger to a spidery scrawl on the plastered sides of the entrance to the barn. In careful script, using what looks like a pencil, someone has written, 'I am planting beans but the rain is heavy and so I am sheltering here. 3 May 1943.' And further down 'Antonio Barbieri 31 July 1942, I am threshing the grain', 'I am standing

here in the afternoon. 21 October 1943. I am waiting to collect the maize. It is raining.'

'Who was he?' I ask, but Rinuccia doesn't know. '*L'uomo*,' she replies, meaning simply the man. There is the sense that the man, whoever he was, expected to get into trouble from his master if he didn't explain why he was not working at a particular moment of the day.

We go to another building that once served as a stable. Rinuccia is keen to show me the place where a cow broke loose and smashed a wooden drinking trough. It's still lying there on the musty scraps of hay, broken into pieces. It happened a long time ago but she is full of indignation when she thinks of the cow.

We go down through the terraced vineyard towards the grand house where Rinuccia lives all on her own. We stop to look at the twisted branches of two mulberry trees planted by the old Engineer. One bears a red fruit and the other a white. We look at a tree I am told is very rare and comes from Sicily, but I don't recognise it and Rinuccia has forgotten its name.

97

Now we are in front of the little chapel built for the *padrone*'s family, with just enough room for a couple of short rows of them to sit and face the priest and the altar. A heraldic shield carved in white stone is set above the door: two fat cockerels confronting each other, each with a clawed foot raised in what might be a greeting but looks more like the first stages in a fight to the death. The date above the cockerels is 1602.

'You must want to see the house!' says Rinuccia, but neither of us seems sure if this is true. She pushes open her own front door and we both walk in tentatively like visitors whose arrival has not been announced. The hallway is hidden in a partial darkness and the blinds are drawn in the first room we enter. I can just distinguish a glass cabinet filled with rifles and a sombre painting of the Holy Family.

'*Il padrone*,' says Rinuccia by way of explanation and she leads me to the kitchen where the shutters are open to reveal a wide expanse of tiled floor shining like a pool of water, a little table, a single chair and a gas cooker. I don't see any cupboards and I don't even see any personal items: a vase, a clock, a string of garlic. Even here in a room that is obviously used there is no sense of the place being inhabited, but neither is it abandoned because everything is spotlessly clean with not a trace of dust or the drifting strand of a spider's web.

Rinuccia turns and leads me back outside, and the visit is brought to an abrupt end. I shake her hand and thank her, and she snorts and tells me that next time she will show me the *padrone*'s collection of photographs. She says she will look for the picture of Benedetta the beggar woman and the one of Old Tunin in which you can see how much he resembles his master. 'Heh!' she says, and rubs her two fingers against each other in case I haven't quite understood her meaning.

Later, when I see the photograph, the two men are indeed the same height and they share the same eyes and foreheads. A dead wild boar lies stretched

out on the ground in front of them, its legs bound and its head close to the feet of the *padrone*. There is an expression of tense and stifled anger in Old Tunin's face and a smug complacency in the face of the *padrone*. Little Tunin stands between them. He can't be more than twelve years old. He has a rifle on one shoulder and a dead hare on the other, and he looks very pleased with himself, bursting with that same energy and excitement that he still has today, almost eighty years later.

I describe to Adriana all the things Rinuccia has shown me and she is very impressed. 'I think it might be the first time she has gone into the House of the Stair by herself,' she says. 'And she has never shown me the door the soldiers tried to break down or the place where the cow damaged the wooden trough. I have heard about them, of course, but the house and everything around it belongs to the *padrone*.

'Old Tunin's father was a tiny man, smaller than me and bent double with that illness which can now be cured. People said of him that he had "seen all the colours" and that was because of his wife. She knew nothing of the world except obedience and the *padrone* said to her, "First you do the hoeing and then you come with me!" and so she went with him because he was her master and she belonged to him. It gave Tunin's father a bad heart and made him nervous. That is what people meant when they said he had seen all the colours.'

# A Funeral

I had meant to visit Rinuccia again, but I think I was a bit nervous of her and that was why I kept putting it off.

She had been very welcoming. 'Come,' she had said, 'and I will show you the photographs, and I will tell you stories, oh, such stories about the war and the things I have seen.'

And then suddenly that tough and determined lady was lying in hospital and once she was there she never came back. She had been feeling unwell, but she said nothing about it until she couldn't walk because of the pain and an ambulance came and took her away.

The doctors were sure it was nothing serious. She just needed a little operation after which she should recover quickly. But she got all sorts of complications and I heard that even if she had been able to leave the hospital she had become too weak ever to be able to manage by herself in the big, isolated house that had been her home for so long.

Eliana went to visit her in hospital and she showed Rinuccia her swelling, pregnant belly. Rinuccia touched the tight skin with her hand and said how pleased she was about the baby coming, but she also said she knew she would never live to see it. She died a few days later.

It was a strange funeral because the family of the *padrone* were there as well as the people from the village and it was like two clans, walking along the road close together but with their hackles raised. The coffin was laden with huge wreaths of artificially bright flowers and I thought of Rinunccia lying inside it, her composed, weatherbeaten, beautiful face, her short grey hair pulled back with grips, her ankle socks and strong shoes and the skirt reaching just below her knees. And then I could see the carefully buttoned man's waistcoat and I was tempted to place one hand across her breast and to put a bunch of wood anemones and wild violets in the waistcoat's upper pocket.

# Old Tunin

In 1988, when he was in his nineties, Adriana's father-in-law, Old Tunin, told the story of his life to a journalist and his account was published in a little book with a photograph of him smoking a pipe on the cover. Adriana has lent me her copy.

Old Tunin is made to express himself in an elaborate and flowery style, which doesn't sound very real, but I never heard him speak, so I can't be sure:

> Under what moon was I born? . . . under the moon which helps the beans
> to grow and allows or cuts short the growth of Christians . . . I think I must

have been born under a moon of war, because men call me *the man of four wars*.

I am known as Tunin da Muta, because of my wife who is deaf and dumb. People say I must have good fortune with a woman who is silent, but I didn't marry her for that reason, I married her because she is as strong as our mountains.

He talks of his childhood, but he doesn't mention the house in which he was born or the baskets filled with chestnut leaves under which he slept when it was raining. He doesn't talk of the *padrone* who had probably sired him and who was responsible for his unusually tall frame and the shape of his eyebrows and forehead.

Old Tunin explains that he was taken out of school when he was eight years old. He had got into trouble for rolling a wooden ball across the classroom floor during a lesson. The teacher complained to his father, who was delighted and said, 'Good! No more school for him then. Now he can work along with the rest of us!' and that was that.

From May until September, or later if the weather was good, Old Tunin's family, like so many other families in the village, needed to graze their goats and sheep and perhaps a cow or two on the pastures on the crest of the mountains, where the land belonged to nobody. In order to survive through the year they also needed to grow extra crops there, wheat and potatoes, beans and grapes. But at the same time they had to go on serving the *padrone*, so they lived double lives, working for the master by day and for themselves in the hours of dusk and dawn and by the light of a full moon. From one generation to the next they built and maintained rough houses for themselves in remote and inaccessible places, and from one generation to the next they sculpted the steepest land into cultivated terraces. You can still see the walls, like traces of some lost civilisation.

One child, usually the youngest and so the most easily spared, was chosen to look after the animals and the land through the summer months. Old Tunin, and then his son Arturo; Armando, Giovanin the shepherd, they were all put in charge of their family's mountain dwellings from the age of eight. They tended the animals and walked the high pastures with them through the day; in the evening they brought them back to the shelter of a building and milked them and made cheese and ricotta. Then they fed the dogs and cooked their own simple meals and watered the crops growing on the terraces. When it was time for the wheat to be cut or the grapes to be harvested, most of the family would come for a few days, although some only had time to work through the night and they were gone again before the dawn.

The land used by Old Tunin's family was at a place known as Carmo, right on the crest of the mountain and a steep two or three hours' walk from the House of the Stair. Old Tunin looked after three cows and five goats; sometimes his elder brother was with him as well. He had to travel a long way to get to a good area for grazing and then he was expected to stay out for several days, sleeping in one of the little stone huts built by the shepherds. Some of the children might be allowed to come back to their family in the evening, but they were punished if they arrived before the night had fallen. When it was suddenly too dark to see the path home you could hold on to the tail of a cow to guide you.

Old Tunin learnt how to make traps to catch small birds and he remembered the delight of catching his first badger and roasting it over a fire. There were other boys on the mountains, but they were not supposed to make contact with each other, for fear that their animals might get mixed up. Some of them found the solitude impossible to bear and it scarred them for life.

Old Tunin said that this was when the pleasure of hunting first got into his blood and it never left him. As a young man he went out hunting with the Engineer who was maybe his father and later he went on his own, walking up into the snow-covered mountains and staying away for several days on end. He shot the fat whistling marmots and the pretty chamois with their elegant striped faces and a tendency to make a sneezing noise when surprised. He also shot hares and badgers for food, and foxes, polecats and wolves for their fur.

Adriana told me that all the men from the valley who had managed to catch wolves had the tails stitched to the capes they wore at the big annual fairs where they would bring their skins to be sold. Old Tunin was famous throughout the valley, because he always had so many skins to sell.

In the early part of the last century there were no wild pigs in this part of Italy, but then around 1937 or '38 there was a big fire that spread through the forests and mountains in the south-east of France and the wild pigs escaped over the high passes and came here. According to his book, Old Tunin was out hunting marmot when he saw unfamiliar tracks in the snow. He followed the tracks and caught a glimpse of the dark bulk of a huge beast. He didn't manage to kill it, but he brought back the story of what he had seen.

Then the war came and the men who were too old to be called up as soldiers hid their old guns in caves or holes in terrace walls, in spite of the penalty for doing so, and they worried about their sons who had been taken away from them and might never come back. Then after the total collapse of the government in September 1943, when the whole country was in turmoil, many of the sons who did manage to return became partisan fighters. Their fathers gave them what weapons they had and helped them to find hiding places in the forests and mountains, and brought food for them when they could and sometimes joined them for a while.*

For those final two years of the war, everyone was too busy hunting the human enemy to bother about anything else but once the war was over Old Tunin organised his partisan friends into military-style squadrons and they went after the wild pig with the same eager determination that they had previously used against the Fascists.

'Hunting wild pigs is just a continuation of the war,' says Adriana. 'The men like to dress up like partisans and then they take their guns into the mountains. There have been accidents in which one man was killed by another, or at least I hope they were accidents, but now it is more ordered

*Italy entered the war on 10 June 1940. In July 1941 62,000 Italian troops were sent to the Eastern Front, their number growing to 200,000 by a year later. They suffered heavy losses at Stalingrad and were withdrawn by the summer of 1943. In July 1943 Mussolini was overthrown by General Badoglio and King Victor Emmanuel III, who signed a secret armistice with the Allies. When the Germans discovered this they moved quickly to disarm Italian troops and took over crucial strategic areas. Mussolini was rescued by the Germans in September 1943 and set up a new Fascist state in northern Italy. At this point the first partisan formations came into being and they resisted the Fascists, both German and Italian, until the end of the war in Italy in May 1945. Liguria was one of the areas where the partisans fought most fiercely.

and you have to wear a luminous vest, so no one can say he mistook you for a pig.'

Old Tunin died at the age of ninety-six. You can see the photograph of him with his pipe and Turin his hunting dog in a couple of local restaurants and in the houses of his descendants. The league of hunters that he founded arranged for a memorial to be made for him, with a bronze image based on the photograph. The memorial was erected at a high pass in the mountains and on the anniversary of his death his descendants organise a big feast and people come to eat and drink and talk together and play a loud game called *moro*, which involves a lot of shouting and the slapping of fists on tables. The priest is there to officiate, a plastic cup filled with wine in one hand and a cigarette in the other, and at a certain point he puts on his white robes and gives a sermon about this life and the life hereafter, standing in front of Old Tunin's memorial and so entranced by the ponderous music of his own voice that he finds it hard to stop.


27 January 2006 (from my notebook):
Deep snow in the morning. The quiet of it and the mountains hanging like tapestries; the warp and the woof of the trees and paths.

I try to find my own quiet. A jug, a bowl, orange oranges, green rosemary, the tick of the stove, the drip of icy water melting in the dark night outside. It is time for me to learn to not be afraid.


23 February 2006
Snow and hailstones and wild winds. I wonder whether to write things about being here: the weather, the creatures, the people, the small doings of the day.


20 March 2006
A reddish-brown frog in the water tank with a little dark frog on her back. Two clumps of spawn – an image of the returning new year more vivid than bulbs pushing through the ground.

20 April 2006
The golden-eyed toad struggling with his arms in the spirals of water weed.
Frogs, so easily confused with princes. Yesterday I saw a hoopoe in the cemetery.

# A Supper Party

This is a celebration of Armando's eighty-second birthday and it's being
held in the house of his daughter and son-in-law. I have seen Armando
often enough to recognise him from a distance and to wave a greeting, but
I have never spoken to him before.

We are all gathered around the table and he arrives late because he was
feeding the goats and chickens. He says that anyway he had some pasta
before he left, so he is not hungry. He is not thirsty either. He sits in a chair
by the fire, his little dog on his lap. He is tall and good-looking in spite of
his age, with a fine set of what must surely be false teeth, which often flash
a smile. He is darker skinned than most of the people here, which earned
him the name 'the black one'.

We have salami and cheese and bread and tagliatelli with a sauce made
from wild mushrooms, and a rabbit stew with olives and white wine and
red wine. Armando sits and watches us as we eat and drink. His daughter
produces a birthday cake she has made for him.

'At least have some of this,' she says, and after a bit of prevarication he
agrees to cut the first slice and to make a wish and to keep quiet about the
nature of the wish so as not to spoil its magic.

His daughter divides the rest of the cake and says that for her part she
wishes for all of us to become as old as he is and as strong. 'How do you
do it?' she asks.

'Patience,' he says with a private grin. 'You need patience in order to
live.'

We all clink our glasses in a toast. 'Chin chin,' we say and then we eat the cake. Armando has been almost silent but now he starts to talk. His words rush into each other in short fast sentences and it's as if he is thinking aloud and is not aware that anyone is listening.

'A family arrived in the village,' he says. 'This was before the war. Nobody knew who they were or where they had come from. They took the house next to where I lived with my brother and my mother and father. The house was not good. It had no windows and the roof was broken because it had been empty for a long time. The family slept on hay. They made a fire in the middle of the room when it was cold.

'There was a table on the terrace in front of the house. Sometimes the family put out plates and glasses and pans and sat round the table. They banged their knives on the plates. They clinked their glasses and said "chin chin". But the plates and the glasses were empty because they had no food to eat, no wine to drink.

'They shouted very loudly to make sure we came out to watch them. "Look at us!" they shouted. "We are eating just like the rich people do! We are enjoying ourselves, just like the rich people do!" Then they pretended to eat and pretended to drink and when they had finished their meal of nothing, they sang a loud song before going back inside the house.'

Armando was not sure when the family went away, but he thought it was during the first year of the war. They didn't say goodbye and after a while the house collapsed completely and people used the stones for other things, so now you can't even see where it used to be.

I go to visit Armando a few days later. He carries his age lightly, even though he says that his back aches all the time and one knee is swollen so he walks with a slight hobble. He lives in the house of his childhood but he says it has been modernised so much it's not the same place at all apart from the sound of the river, which has not changed. Ida, his sister-in-law, lives in the house next door. They are more or less the same age and they were both recently widowed. These days they sit together sometimes and Ida might present him with a piece of pie she has made or he might give her a bottle of his own wine. In the past they avoided each other even though they were so physically close that it must have taken a lot of effort. It was something to do with an old quarrel, which was only resolved a few months before the death of the two main protagonists.

'We are in Ida's kitchen. It has a shiny tiled floor and a shiny formica table and a long shiny wooden sideboard along one wall and a glass door to the outside terrace with a lace curtain to keep out the glare of the sunlight. Armando has his little dog on his lap and Ida's marmalade cat sits on the floor and watches it. Ida shows me a framed photograph of her husband, which she takes from the sideboard. He is very handsome and his lips have been given a red tint. We all agree that he looks like a Hollywood filmstar.

Armando has brought a bottle of his wine. He pours some into his glass and takes a sip. 'No good!' he says, pushes the dog from his lap and gets up to empty the contents of the bottle down the sink. He finds a new bottle, the dog returns to its place and we begin again. 'Chin chin!'

Neither he nor Ida can get a good night's sleep any more. Ida takes pills, while Armando lies awake and thinks about the past. He says he remembers nothing of his life after the war was over, but before then he sees everything, 'just like watching a film on television'.

He says he has often thought of writing things down, but there seemed no point. Now he thinks he would like to write them and give them to me. It will be something to do during the hours of wakefulness.

He talks very fast and keeps lapsing into the local dialect; Ida interrupts him to tell him to stick to Italian or to explain to me what he has been saying. Sometimes she touches his shoulder to keep him quiet while she translates his words.

He talks about going to school before the war and how all the village children had to appear in the square on Saturday wearing white shirts and with a black flower in their hats. If they failed to give the Fascist salute, they were made to drink castor oil. Even the adults were made to drink the oil if they didn't show the right enthusiasm for the man they called The Lion.

'Mussolini wanted all our saucepans so he could melt them down and turn them into guns, to use in his war in Abyssinia. But we hid ours, because without a saucepan a family cannot eat and is nothing. He wanted our guns as well, but we hid them too. We had hiding places everywhere, in the walls of terraces, in hollow trees and in the caves.'

I am not sure how the jump is made, but suddenly he is telling me about Clelia, the daughter of the bonesetter, who became a bonesetter herself. 'Clelia was very strong,' says Armando. 'She went on working on the land until she was ninety-three, but now she has lost her mind. Her daughter looks after her.'

'She is a strange girl, the daughter,' says Ida. 'Her father died and she was sent to live with her grandfather in the high village, and when she came back here she remained silent for years. She was pretty, but she never had a boyfriend.'

'A very rich lady, whose leg was so crooked she couldn't walk, came to see Clelia,' says Armando, ignoring Ida's interruption. 'She was carried in on a chair and Clelia knelt down in front of her and felt all the bones with her fingers,' and Armando leans forward to make the gesture of feeling bones with his own fingers.

'Then Clelia said, "Hold still! This will make you cry!"' and Armando makes a quick chopping movement with the side of his hand to show how Clelia hit the leg.

'"Now, stand up!"' says Armando, as if he were Clelia talking, and he and Ida both look in front of them and seem to see the rich lady rising from the chair that had carried her and standing there straight-legged, with tears of gratitude pouring down her cheeks.

'That was Clelia!' says Armando emphatically.

'Yes, that was Clelia!' agrees Ida.

# Clelia and Her Sister

A few years ago we were walking the path from Adriana's house down to the village when we heard soft chattering voices. We rounded a bend and there in a little patch of a vineyard were two extremely old and extremely tiny ladies busy with the vines. One of them was standing on a stepladder with a pair of secateurs in her hand and her cotton skirt pulled up over her head and shoulders to give protection from the sun. That was Clelia. The other was holding the stepladder and she had removed her blouse to reveal a solid-looking bra. That was Clelia's older sister. They greeted us and laughed at being discovered in such a state of undress and Clelia pulled her skirt back into place, but with no sense of embarrassment.

'We are tired of pruning!' they said, and in my recollection they spoke in a single voice.

'Of course they are tired of it!' said Adriana when I told her of this meeting. 'They have been pruning those vines every year since they were little girls, so this must be the ninetieth season for them.'

Then I heard that they had stopped working on the land and that Clelia's sister had gone to bed and refused to get up ever again. She lay there in a motionless bundle and shouted in a loud voice by night and by day. Clelia went on doing things but she was becoming demented and restless, and she only wanted to walk, so she and her daughter went out on regular little expeditions to the cemetery or to the shop. Clelia walked very slowly, holding her daughter tightly by the hand. I sometimes stopped to talk to them and there was a look of permanent surprise tinged with fear on both their faces.

Clelia died just a few weeks ago, early in March 2010, but her sister, who has reached the age of ninety-eight, is still in bed. Ida goes to visit her quite regularly. 'She is so tiny. You wouldn't believe anyone could be so tiny,' she says. 'Her head looks no bigger than an orange and she is all folded up with her face to the wall. She never moves, so it's hard to believe she is really alive.'

I sometimes see the daughter walking back along the road from the cemetery. Her big round eyes surmounted by big black eyebrows are always fixed in that look of fearful surprise and when I greet her she stares at me but doesn't smile or say anything.

And now I've just been told that her ninety-two-year-old aunt has been sent to live with her because she was in hospital and can't manage on her own any more.

# Armando's Pages

I begin to really enjoy these meetings with Armando and Ida. There is not the sense of closeness that I have with Adriana or with her sparkling daughter, but there is the sense of being invited to join them as they step over into the past and look around and see what there is to see and who is there to keep them company.

The next time I come on a visit, Armando presents me with a bundle of pages torn from an A4 notebook. I thank him and take the pages home with me. He writes with a blue biro and his handwriting is steady and precise, in perfect Italian, which is odd since he doesn't like to speak it, and with very few crossings out. He doesn't do paragraphs and there is no punctuation from the start to the finish of his text.

Armando opens with an account of the old way of life here in the village: the people cultivating land that belonged to the rich families, the cotton and thread factory by the river, which later became the military barracks; the chalk-burning pits that were used for making lime; the charcoal burners – wild-looking men who came here every year from the town of Bergamo and worked for ten days in the mountains and then they were gone – the lavender harvest, the chestnut harvest, the hay harvest, the sowing of winter grain, the grape harvest; church processions; people sitting around the fire at night during the winter, telling stories and singing songs.

And then suddenly the pastoral scene vanishes and the spell of lyrical nostalgia is broken. 'All this came to an end in 1940,' writes Armando, 'when we heard the first rumours of war.'

Italy entered the war in June 1940. There was an immediate fear that the valley would be bombed by the French. A government order was issued and the entire population was told they were to be transported to Milan for safety's sake. They must get ready to leave at once.

'I'll let you imagine what confusion there was among the people, so

giornale radio, si sapeva che l'esercito Italiano aveva
deposto le armi, il Re Vittorio Emanuele era fuggito dell'Italia
il regime fascista si era alleato con le forze tedesche che
operavano in Italia i quali avevano preso presidio
di tutti i punti strategici del nord Italia. Intanto gli
americani sbarcati al sud Italia creavano un'altro fronte,
i tedeschi rastrellavano soldati del disfatto esercito per poi
mandarli a combattere sui vari fronti, difficile per le migliaia
di poveri soldati ormai allo sbando che cercavano di fare
ritorno alle loro case e alle loro famiglie, a centinaia i catturati
dai tedeschi e mandati nei campi di concentramento
in Germania e mai più tornati e fra questi molti nostri
compaesani, erano tanti di questi poveri giovani che arrivava-
no da cima Marta fronte francese e passavano nei
nostri paesi in cerca di un pezzo di pane e di vestiti borghesi
per non essere riconosciuti e molto ha fatto la popolazione
per aiutarli. Tristi giorni tristi momenti abbiamo passato
da quel 8 settembre, non si sapeva più notizie dei nostri
padri dei nostri fratelli, si cominciava a formare le prime
bande partigiane detti "Patrioti" si organizzavano
raccogliendo armi e munizioni nelle caserme abbandonate
nella fabbriscie di Vallecrosia. Che erano i Partigiani??
erano i nostri padri e nostri fratelli, tutti noi stessi di
questi paesi imitisi ai molti soldati del disciolto esercito
che non hanno più fatto ritorno alle loro case.
Prime battaglie nelle nostre valli contro i nazisti. I partigiani
meno organizzati operavano egualmente in montagna
per meglio difendersi e nascondersi, operavano in piccoli
gruppi guidati da un capo. Intanto i nazifascisti aprirono
preso presidio a Camporosso nella vecchia fabrica di
cotone e a Molini nelle caserme militari; quasi ogni
giorno perquisivano le nostre case portando via quello
che ci serviva, patate olio, conigli, capretti e quant'altro,
accusandoci di essere protettori dei partigiani; ed era
veramente vero. Un giorno di Giugno i Partigiani hanno

attached to the soil, to their houses and livestock,' writes Armando, sitting propped up in his bed in the middle of the night.

Most of them had never left the village in all their lives and they were very afraid. They had to leave their animals and their crops, which was something they could not imagine doing. Everyone was allowed to take just a single piece of luggage. We had no suitcases so we wrapped things up in cloth. Six hundred and fifty of us gathered in the church square. Imagine the weeping children, the screaming women, the shouting men, the old people fainting from fear.

The village priest did his best to keep us calm and he travelled with us. We were taken on military lorries to the railway station and from there we were bundled into closed goods wagons as if we were cattle being taken to market. It took two days to reach the city of Milan and then we had to wait for ten more hours in the station hall, before being given food to eat and mattresses to sleep on.

Imagine, people like us, who had always lived in our own way, suddenly finding ourselves controlled by military discipline. It was terribly upsetting. As luck would have it, after about twenty days, the order came for us to return to our homes because a treaty had been agreed on with the French.

We left Milan in the middle of the night and this time we made the journey in second-class carriages. On the evening of the next day we were back in our village, anxious to get to our houses, fearful of what we might find.

My dog Alpina had worn a deep circle in the ground from walking round and round on her chain and a chicken with eleven chicks was close to her and I don't know why, but this made me cry. My father dug up the wine he had buried in a big demijohn bottle and my mother dug up her saucepans and some dry food.

But the war went on, now not only against the English and the Americans, but also against the Russians. We worried because so many young men from here had been sent to fight on the Russian front or in various battle zones and we had no news from them. The women took over and confronted the summer of hard work.

I see Armando a few days later, busy with his goats, and I tell him I enjoyed reading his pages very much. 'Thank you,' he says formally, 'I have more for you. I will give it to you the next time you come to my house.'

# Seeing Tuvo

Armando comes to visit us one hot day in the summer. He knows the house well, because he used to be good friends with the old grandfather who lived here.

He clambers quickly out of his car and stalks around on bent legs. 'Ha!' he says triumphantly, looking at the outside steps that have not changed one bit. 'Ha!' he says again, peering into our bathroom, which was where the grandfather had kept thirty sheep.

He explains that the family moved away in 1945, after a man was found dead on a terrace and people said he had been shot, and maybe he had. But the grandfather didn't want to leave entirely, so he still kept his sheep here and grew vines and a few vegetables, and Armando came to help him whenever he could.

We are standing outside in the sunshine, looking towards the mountains on the other side of this part of the valley. Armando asks if we have bin-

oculars and when we bring him a pair he puts them to his eyes and moves them about, searching for something on the opposite slope.

'There it is, there is Tuvo!' he says at last, pointing into the distance where the land is at its most precipitous.

He hands me the binoculars. I can see the grey face of a steep bluff of rock and a blur of spruce trees and rough vegetation, but I am not quite sure what I am looking for.

'Tuvo!' says Armando. 'Where we lived during the summer' – and he begins to lead me through the details of the landscape. 'Go down from that ridge, the sharp one with the shadow, now pass below the five pines and move a little way over to the left. There is the outside wall with a window. Can't you see it?'

I find myself looking at what appears to be a slab of grey rock, but in its upper section I can just distinguish a dark square, which I suppose must be the window.

'That's it!' says Armando, when I describe the square. He takes the binoculars and holds them again to his eyes, but then he puts them quickly away because he is crying, the tears wet on his cheeks. 'We were happy there,' he says, smiling apologetically.

# Adriana Goes to Milan

Adriana was only five when the war began, but she says she has also not forgotten that day when the villagers had to leave. The priest and Pepina came to visit her family by the river to tell them to get ready.

'Pepina?' I have not heard of Pepina.

'She was his housekeeper, but really she was more like his wife; his *perpetua* is what we call it.'

Adriana thinks that Pepina was fifteen when the priest first brought her here from a village further up the valley, although others say she was fourteen, thirteen, or perhaps even twelve. There was certainly a complaint from the bishop because she was so young and very pretty too, with a mass of dark curly hair, but still the priest insisted that this girl was the one he had chosen and he would have no other. He hung his priest's robes outside the window of his bedroom to show he was prepared to give up his life in the Church if it came to that and after a while the complaint was forgotten.

Everyone loved Pepina because she was very jolly and hard-working and full of talk, and she looked after the priest so well. And they all loved the priest because he was like one of them: fishing, hunting, harvesting the olives and growing his own potatoes and beans, and helping them through difficult times with practical things alongside the prayers. He was like one of them in his poverty as well and at Easter he and Pepina would walk to all the houses in the village and he would bless the houses and in return people gave him food: a few eggs, some chestnuts, a cabbage. Pepina put them in the sack that she carried and that helped them through the year. And during the winter, when he hadn't enough fuel for his fire, he would finish Mass and ask if anyone would like to help him collect wood. Pepina never bore him any children but they were together from 1934 until his death in 1966.

After the priest had died Pepina said she wanted to go back to her own village, even though he had made arrangements for her to stay on in the place where they had always lived next to the church, but she was quite decided. Armando says he drove her as far as the road would go and then they walked, carrying her few possessions, which included a big framed photograph of the priest.

Armando was sure she only survived for a year after that because she was so sad, but then someone else told me he saw her just after she died and that must have been in 1990. The undertaker had asked him to help with a funeral and there was little Pepina, lying in her coffin all dressed in white, and he got quite a shock, because he hadn't been told it was her they were burying. She was much fatter than he remembered, but she was still unmistakably herself.

Anyway, back in June 1940, the priest and Pepina made the slow journey on foot, following the paths that connected one house to the next, telling everyone to present themselves at the church square in three days' time. It was a government order and they must obey.

Adriana's father was somewhere far away in the mountains, working with a group of men who were too old to fight and had been sent to repair the road close to the French border. So he couldn't come with them. Her mother cried when she was told to get ready – but then she always cried very easily. She asked how could she look after two little girls without a husband to help her and she looked at Adriana and said it would be different if she had been born a boy. 'You are my misfortune,' she said.

Some people did manage to stay behind. There was an old man living close to the House of the Sea Captain where Adriana lives now and he announced that he wasn't leaving, no matter what the government said; anyone could bring their livestock to him, or at least their cows, and he would do his best to take care of them. Ida's family and three other families from her part of the upper village couldn't get out of their beds because they were very sick with measles, and there were others who were too old to move or they lived in such remote houses that no one managed to reach them with the order.

Everyone else set about like harvest mice, burying their supplies of food and wine and saucepans, and collecting sad little bundles of possessions with no idea of what they might need for such an unfamiliar adventure.

Adriana says she was afraid even before the journey started, but her uncle Modesto promised to look after her and she was glad about that. He was the only man in this part of the valley who had a car, although it was more like an open truck and he used it to collect milk. He was very tall and strong. He held her hand as they walked up the track beside the river to the church square. He carried a sack on his back and he said he could carry her too, if she got tired.

Adriana doesn't remember the bus journey or the train journey, except that the priest and Pepina were busy comforting people and trying to keep them calm, but the station in Milan with its metal roof as big as the sky is still vivid in her mind.

'Uncle Modesto carried me on his shoulders as if he were Saint Christopher,' she says. Whenever the sirens sounded she pressed her face into the rough cloth of his jacket.

She thinks they were gone for two or perhaps three weeks, then they were brought back and life went on as it always had, even though food was increasingly scarce and aeroplanes appeared like dark birds overhead, on their way to bomb towns and cities. She saw the sky go red when the bombs were dropped on San Remo.

———————————

The phone rings and Adriana answers it, whispering into the plastic mouth-piece as if it were an ear brought close to her lips. She stands in a corner of the kitchen, beneath a painted plaque showing a head of Christ wearing the crown of thorns, the blood trickling down the side of his face. 'Hello?' she says querulously. 'Yes, no, yes, yes, thank you, goodbye' and she stares suspiciously at the instrument in her hand before returning it to its cradle on the wall.

'That was the man who comes to help me with the chestnuts,' she says. 'He will be here very soon, so I can't talk any longer. I am sorry. Come and see me another day.'

# An Abandoned House

Recently some friends bought a house in the village of Pepina's childhood; a long thin house with wooden balconies looking out across a steeply wooded valley and filled to the brim with old furniture and all sorts of other possessions that had accumulated over the generations. Everything was there and covered with dust and mouse droppings and the other accretions of time: piles of newspapers from the 1950s, coffee pots without their lids, a bicycle without its wheels, a blackened drying rack for chestnuts, blackened cauldrons for hanging over an open fire, a metal container with leather shoulder straps for carrying water.

Before the house was cleared I went to spend a day there on my own, moving from room to room, making notes and taking photographs, in search of any floating stories I might find.

The wind-up alarm clock in the little kitchen had stopped at 1.34. There were seven threadbare cardigans hanging from hooks on the door and sixteen saucepan lids displayed on the wall above the electric cooker. All the shelves in the two dressers were crowded with unlikely combinations of items: jars of pickled cherries next to a Delcom stereo cassette player in its blue-and-white box; a bottle of something called Elixir Aurora 30% proof, next to a bottle of Jet Balsam shampoo and a spray can of Neocid insecticide. There was a postcard from Lourdes and an ashtray with a printed picture of a boat in the sunset. There was a photograph of a lean-faced smiling man called Antonio who was born in 1941 and died in 1976, and a book for the service of the dead inscribed in ink in big and careful capital letters by 'the second child of Giuseppe' and dated 3 February 1932.

I moved through the upper level of the house, looking at spinning wheels and rat traps, broken three-legged stools and big green glass jars for olives, barrels for wine and rotting cane baskets for collecting fruit.

The rooms below the kitchen were crammed with rickety beds, double and single, and children's beds with hardly enough room to circumnavigate

between them. All the beds were made up with blankets and pillows, as if the ghosts of the past returned at night and climbed in under the musty sheets.

I opened the doors of a wardrobe in which a tiny man's suit was hanging next to some cotton dresses. I opened the drawers of various cupboards and in one I found a printed image of the Holy Family with a scattering of rusty jewellery lying on top of it. In another there was a school report – or *Pagella Scolastica* – for 1928–1929, which charted the uncertain progress of an eight-year-old girl called Filippina. She was given 2 out of 10 for her proficiency in religion, handwriting, cleanliness, conduct and reading 'in the Italian language', and 3 out of 10 for arithmetic, handicrafts, gymnastics and something called *nozioni varie*. The teacher had signed the report without comment and it had also been given an official stamp by the Department of Education.

There was something so poignant about this brief record of a young life that I took it with me when I left the house, putting it in a plastic bag along with a curiously random assortment of other papers and photographs, shopping lists and postcards and the battered pages of an illustrated romantic novel from the 1950s. Then some months later Armando and Ida were talking about their school reports, so I took it to show them.

They looked at the familiar Fascist-royalist insignia on the outside cover and at the name and surname of the pupil and the date of her birth, and they both said this must be the priest's Pepina, of course it is, it can't be anyone else. They laughed at how bad her marks were, but then what could you expect, her family was poor and she had so much other work to do apart from attending school.

# La Muta

'I have found some pictures to show you,' says Adriana when I am with her again. She goes to the next room and returns holding two photographs, which she puts on the table in front of me. They are half postcard size, with serrated edges.

'This is La Muta, the Silent Woman. She was like a mother to me and much kinder to me than my own mother,' she says. 'You see how tall she is and how elegant. She is wearing one of her own dresses.'

In the other photograph La Muta stands next to her husband Old Tunin. I would guess that she was in her fifties when the photo was taken. Dark cotton dress, hair pulled back from her face and a serious expression as she confronts the camera. She is the same height as Old Tunin, but I don't know how tall he was.

La Muta was born in a tiny village even higher up the mountain than the village of Adriana's father. She tells me that her house had three floors, which made it unusual, and the year 1865 was scratched into the long stone lintel above the door. Adriana says that no one lives there now because it is too difficult to reach, so the roof has probably fallen in and maybe the building is nothing more than a heap of rubble.

La Muta's real name was Maietta. When she was four years old she fell ill with measles. She recovered, but something was clearly wrong with her because she had become frightened and she didn't respond to the voices of her family. It was only when her mother asked the doctor to come that they understood that the child was deaf. He arranged for her to be taken to a convent school in the town of Imperia where they had done a lot of work with deaf children. She remained there for almost twenty years and I don't think her parents were ever able to visit her.

The nuns taught La Muta how to lip-read, but they never encouraged her to try to speak because that was not the policy of their school. Much later when she needed to try to speak because no one around her could lip-read, the voice that emerged had a peculiar honking flatness and the sounds she made had no recognisable form to them. But her parents learnt to understand her and so did her children and her grandchildren.

She was a bright pupil and when the nuns taught her how to read she read all the books of the New Testament until she knew them by heart, line by line, page by page, chapter by chapter. She also learnt how to sew a fine stitch and she could make beautiful dresses for ladies and even more beautiful trousers for men. It was probably expected that in return for such an education, La Muta would agree to become a member of the convent, but she must have refused, because when she was twenty-one she returned to the valley and to the house of her parents, like a stranger from another world.

Even though she could lip-read she had forgotten the local dialect, so she couldn't understand what people were saying to her, unless they communicated in simple Italian. She could recite passages from the books of the Evangelists, but no one knew how to disentangle the awkward sounds she produced in an imitation of words. That was when she became known as La Muta, the Silent Woman.

La Muta worked with her parents and other members of her family in the fields and the chestnut forests and among the vines and olives. She had a strong body and didn't tire easily and in the evening she made clothes. The nuns had taught her how to produce trousers in the old style with the opening at the back and long sashes that were tied tight round the middle. All the men wanted to own a pair like that, which they could wear to funerals or weddings or to church on a Sunday.

When she had just turned thirty, La Muta married Tunin. He was nine years her junior, which made it a very unusual match. When he was interviewed for his book, Tunin sings his wife's praises in very lyrical terms: 'We are equals, she and I, and if I am a wild boar, she is a chamois and the lights of Easter and Christmas are in her eyes,' but Adriana will have none of that and says he took her because he had seen what a hard worker she was and he knew she could always earn extra money by making clothes.

'He was cruel to her,' says Adriana, suddenly upset by his cruelty, 'and he mocked her because she was deaf and because her voice sounded so odd and because she was older than him.'

She remembers La Muta knocking on the door of her house late one night, because of a quarrel. 'Help me, Adriana ... Tunin!' and Adriana imitates the soft, flat voice of her mother-in-law with such an intensity that I can almost see her, standing in the darkness, asking to be let in and given shelter.

Still angry with the thought of Old Tunin, Adriana says he took other women when he could find them and he drank a lot of wine, and the drink brought out his bad temper and made him shout and throw things around.

Sometimes he would take his gun and say he was going to shoot someone, but luckily he never did. But then she softens. 'It was because he was getting old,' she says. 'He was a man who didn't like to get old and La Muta understood that and forgave him everything. And even if he didn't love her as much as he should have, she didn't mind because she had her children and she loved them more than anything in the world.'

La Muta had a daughter and four sons. A fifth son died of bronchitis at the age of eight months. She told Adriana that when she was working on her Singer sewing machine, she kept one foot on the treadle and one on the chest in which her babies slept so she could feel the wood shake if the baby was crying. And when she walked the steep paths to the forests or the pastures, she carried a big cane basket on her head with a baby wrapped up in swaddling bands lying alongside other necessities; she could feel the little body twitching like a chrysalis if it was in distress.

All the women transported their babies like this until they were too big to be swaddled, then they were carried on the back with a cloth holding them steady. When they had arrived at their destination, the women would be busy cutting or digging or harvesting, while the small children were tethered to branches like little goats or watched over by the slightly older ones. I suddenly remember Armando talking about his mother walking the steep and rocky paths, with a basket on her head, a pack on her back, a goat attached to her wrist by a little rope and as she walks she is busy knitting socks. 'They were all like that, the women,' said Armando proudly.

———————————

La Muta's youngest son, Arturo, was eight years old when he fell against a stone and cut his knee very badly. Old Tunin took him to a woman in the village who knew how to deal with such things and she prepared a hot tomato and onion poultice to bind round the wound. Something went badly wrong and the poultice didn't work. By now the wound was septic and Arturo had developed a high fever. Then the leg began to turn black. Arturo never forgot the pain for the rest of his life. He said he saw the Devil standing in front of him and he begged his parents to cut off his leg with an axe, with a knife, with anything, so long as they removed it.

The priest was a good friend of Tunin's and when he was brought to see Arturo, he said the child must go to hospital at once or he would die. He promised to find the money for the treatment, either from his own pocket or from the weekly collections in the church.

Arturo was away for nine months and every week Tunin went on his bicycle to visit his son, four hours there and four hours back. And because the whole family was struggling to survive under such pressure, the priest would often arrange for his congregation to go to Tunin's house after Mass was over, because there was wheat to be planted, grapes to be harvested, wood to be chopped and the *padrone* still needed his share of everything.

Arturo was finally able to come back home, with one leg shorter than the other so he walked with a heavy limp for the rest of his life. The other children teased him and many of the adults avoided him because any kind of physical deformity was seen as a bad omen. From the age of ten until his marriage fourteen years later he was given the responsibility of looking after the sheep and goats, and he was on his own in the high mountains from the beginning of May until the end of September. He said later that the isolation was so extreme that he felt himself slipping away from the human world.

Adriana met La Muta for the first time when they were all hiding from the German soldiers and the Fascists in a stone house high up in the chestnut forest. This was after the attack by the bridge when a number of soldiers had been killed and everyone was terrified of the reprisals that were bound to follow. She remembers La Muta saying '*Ferma, zitta, prega!* (Keep still, keep silent, pray!') by lifting her hands up as if in surprise like the angels painted on the outside wall of the church by the river, putting a finger to her lips and making a shush noise and then placing the palms of her hands together and bowing her head. Adriana says she immediately felt safe with her, even though they were in such danger.

'It was difficult to understand her at first and I was even afraid of the strange noises she made, but then I learnt how to talk to her slowly and clearly and how to read her lips.'

'I can't hear and so I know nothing about the world. Tell me something,' she would say and then Adriana would tell her little things about what she had done on that day or what she was planning to do tomorrow, and she says it was like telling a fairy story to a child because La Muta took so much pleasure from watching the words take shape.

La Muta had a special love for Arturo because of what he had suffered as a child and the loneliness of his life in the mountains, and when Arturo and Adriana lost their first child it was La Muta who comforted them and made them strong. Adriana remembers her coming into the room where they were sitting desolate and weeping. She made a gesture with her hands showing she wanted to sit between them and she put her arms round them and said in her flat voice, 'Now you are like me.'

'She understood what we were going through because she also lost a baby once. When I am dying it will be her face that I see watching over me,' says Adriana.

# As if I Had Known Her

It can sometimes happen that you become so familiar with a person you have never met that you think of them as an old friend even if they died long before you were born.

I have that with La Muta. Instead of inhabiting my imagination she seems to have entered my memory, so that I can see her walking towards me and I can see myself sitting down at a table in her kitchen in the House of the Warm Spring as if I knew the house well. I sit there beside her and look at the careful stitches on the dress she is wearing and watch the changing expressions on her face, which is intense with the need to understand and to be understood. I can hear the flat and plaintive sounds she makes when she tries to speak, but mostly it is her silence that stays with me: conversations that do not need to be translated into words.

---

I used to be very close to a Dutch poet who was born not long after the turn of the last century. She was known to her friends as Kiek, which was a diminutive of Katarina, and she wrote her exquisite and startling poetry under the pen name of Vasalis.

Kiek was a psychiatrist by profession and she had worked in mental wards for much of her life. I remember her saying that she missed the old days before modern sedatives and tranquillisers were being so freely administered because she had got used to working in what she called the noisy kingdom of the mad, a world filled with the screams and roars and babblings of sound, which was so much closer to the reality of these people in a state of crisis than the subdued silences induced by chemicals.

Kiek lived with her husband in a house facing a field in which there were three wild cherry trees standing in a row. One winter there was an ice storm and she woke to see the trees glistening from crown to root and festooned with heavy blossoms of ice. She knew the trees would die, but still it was so beautiful to see them like that and even now, she said, when she looked at their blackened silhouettes, she remembered how they stood that morning in the winter sunshine.

I saw quite a lot of Kiek and her husband during the years when I was living in Holland, and when I returned to England I went to stay with them a few times. I often felt she knew more about me than I had ever told her and I hope I was able to see her with equal clarity. This is an excerpt from the last letter she sent to me, not long before she died. She had just turned ninety and her husband, who outlived her for a few months, was ninety-eight.

*June 1997*

*Thank you so much for your letter – a change in the ink – I start again: I was so glad to hear from you. You did have a very heavy and tricky landscape to travel through, unsheltered, uncharted, a rough and unknown road, but here you are again and you sound good to me. I*

*try to imagine you as you are now and whether I would find any*
*difference in your new work – well I suppose all your writings differ*
*from each other while keeping – thank god – the unmistakable*
*Julia-ness . . . As for us, we are very old now. We feel it and look it,*
*but mainly physically, inwardly we still live completely (though we*
*blunder more often as regards names and periods and are sooner*
*exhausted) but what else can you expect? We still get the messages from*
*that mysterious land in which our roots live – musical or verbal*
*communications from inside one can trust, a mixture of old and*
*newborn thoughts and feelings.*

*I must stop now. Are you ever coming to Holland – I mean for a*
*visit? I don't suppose so, but even if we don't see you again, you are*
*fully present in our thoughts.*

I remember one night when I was very sad about something and I comforted myself by imagining Kiek sitting beside me, and she telephoned me the next day to say she had been thinking about me and she hoped I was all right. Like Adriana with La Muta, I sometimes think it is my old friend's quiet and intense face criss-crossed with a delicate tracery of little lines that I will see when I die.

# Armando's Insomnia

There was no electricity in the village during the war and the only way of getting news was from a radio that belonged to the Engineer who had his own generator.

The priest went to the Engineer's house to listen to the radio, so that he could report back to the villagers and tell them how things were going. On 8 September 1943 he learnt that the Italian government had collapsed and the king had fled the capital along with all his ministers.

A few days later he listened to a broadcast on behalf of the Americans and the English. They had now become the Allies and they said the war was over, or at least almost over. But then there was a new announcement, which explained that the Italian Fascist party was in control of the situation, thanks to the help of the German army, and they were fighting the English and American intruders on all fronts. According to this version of the truth, anyone who deserted from the Italian army would be shot as a traitor.

In his private diary the priest has no illusions about what is to come. He can see that things are going to get much worse before there is any chance of them getting better. He does his best to explain the situation to his congregation, but he cannot hide his sense of deep foreboding. 'God will take care of you now,' he says in his sermon and it is the only comfort he can offer. Everyone hopes that indeed God will take care of them, since it's clear no one else is going to.

———————•———————

Armando props himself up in bed during the long hours of the night and he writes about this period of the war, his blue biro racing along the narrow lines of an A4 notebook:

On 8 September the politicians set in train the chaotic disbanding of the Italian army. At first we didn't know that our army had surrendered and that King Vittorio Emmanuel had fled the country and the Fascist regime had aligned itself with the German forces, which had taken possession of all the strategic points in the north of Italy.

In the meantime, the Americans had landed in the South, creating another battle zone. The Germans rounded up the soldiers from the disbanded Italian army and sent them to fight on various fronts.

Thousands of poor soldiers were wandering around, trying to find a way of returning to their families. Hundreds were captured by the Germans and sent to German concentration camps, never to return. Many poor young men came to our villages in search of a bit of bread and some ordinary clothes so they wouldn't be recognised as soldiers and our people did all they could to help them.

And so the first bands of partisans were formed, calling themselves the Patriots and finding arms and ammunition in the abandoned military barracks of the munitions storehouse in this valley.

Who were the partisans? They were our fathers and brothers; everyone from our villages, along with the many disbanded soldiers who hadn't been able to return to their homes. They worked from the mountains, in order to have a better chance to hide and defend themselves. They operated in small groups under the command of one leader.

My brother had been sent to fight in the war, but I was too young, so I had stayed behind with my parents. After the collapse of the Fascist government, my brother made his way back to the village. He was on a train and an American soldier saw that his shoes were worn out and gave him a new pair and he was very grateful for that.

Armando's brother realised that if he got off at the station he would probably be spotted and arrested immediately as a deserter, so he jumped from the moving train and followed the old footpaths until he reached his family home. Even his father cried when he walked through the door. It was too dangerous for him to stay for more than a couple of days. He went to hide in the mountains along with the other young men who had also become partisans, more by default than from any deep political conviction. Armando stayed at home for the time being.

In the spring of 1944 the German Fascists had taken possession of the old cotton factory down by the river. Almost every day they ransacked our houses, taking whatever they wanted: potatoes, rabbits, oil, baby goats and anything else, while accusing us of being protectors of the partisans, which was true, but we had no choice.

The Fascists suspected that the young men must be hiding somewhere close by. They suspected that Old Tunin knew where they were, so they burnt down his house as a warning and they put up notices saying they would burn other houses as well if these men did not present themselves at the military barracks on the next day. The notices said we would come to no harm if we did as we were told.

It was winter and there was snow on the ground. We were all very afraid. We thought our mothers and fathers would be killed for us if we did not go, so we put on our best shirts and trousers and set off along the road towards the barracks. But on the way we were ambushed by the partisans, who captured us like prisoners and took us to an old barn by the river. They told us to strip naked and they put all our clothes into sacks and even took our shoes, and said, 'Now go and present yourselves to the Fascists!' We were ashamed and couldn't go anywhere and we stayed there by the river all that day and through the night. It was very cold.

But then we learnt that the Fascists had found two young men from the upper village who were hiding in a cave; they had been betrayed by the mark of their own footsteps in the snow. They were bound and led away to be shot and that was too much to bear, so I and my brother and some twenty other young men from this part of the valley walked to the military barracks, naked and on bare feet. I can remember the sentry's look of surprise when he saw us. We let ourselves be taken and we were given army uniforms to wear and we were locked up in a room and kept there for about twenty days, although we were brought out for exercise.

They woke us in the middle of one night and loaded us up like mules. I was made to carry three mortars, rifles and other weapons in a big sack on my back.

We marched until we reached the high village where people come to pasture their animals during the summer, but this was in the winter so the land was covered in snow. That was where two of our young men managed to escape. The Fascists thought we had helped them to get away, so we were forced to walk barefoot in the snow as a punishment, to make us say where they had gone, where they might be hiding. But we knew nothing, so we kept silent.

They eventually gave us back our shoes and we went on walking and after maybe three days we entered the land on the other side of the mountains. We were divided into small groups of five or less, because in that way they thought we couldn't organise ourselves into any sort of resistance. Each group was attached to a platoon of some twenty-five Fascists. We were supposed to be finding the partisans and trying to kill them, but they knew we were on the side of the partisans, so we were not given guns. We tried to keep at the back and out of trouble.

I witnessed one big fight. There was deep snow all around and a sharp wind. At least seven of the Fascist soldiers were killed and it was so cold their corpses were frozen solid. When the fighting was over, I had to help carry these dead men to a barn filled with hay; lifting them was like lifting pieces of wood.

I was told I must spend the night keeping guard over the dead men. I was on my own with them. I was given a lantern and a chair and I sat and watched the corpses lying in hay, and as I watched them their bodies began to thaw. I saw them shuddering with movement as an arm dropped to its side, a head lolled, a leg went limp. It was as if the dead were coming to life complete with all the wounds that had killed them and I was so frightened I pissed in my pants.

One night, in another place, I was with my brother when the partisans came. They threw a stone against the door to let us know they were there and said, 'Come with us! Cut loose from the Fascists! They will order you to kill your own people and they will kill you if you refuse! We know the way back over the mountains. We will lead you to your valley.'

Nine of us agreed to go, the rest were too afraid.

We walked through the darkness until we came to a barn, which held some thirty cows. So we had milk to drink and the bodies of the animals to keep us warm, but while we were sleeping the cows started to eat our shoes.

We could only move under cover of darkness and it took us four or five days to get home, walking through the snow with nothing to eat and only melted snow to drink and nothing to keep us warm. I would never have survived without my older brother who comforted me when I cried and rubbed my feet and wrapped his arms round me while I slept. Finally we reached the familiar ridge of the mountain above our village and I was so excited I slid the last hundred metres down the slope on the snow.

We were covered with sores and lice. Our parents hid us in a hole behind the stove because by now the Fascists were everywhere. We slept like marmots in a cave for several days behind the stove, waking only to eat a bit of soup.

As soon as he felt strong enough my brother went to join the partisans in the forest above the village, but I was afraid and I stayed in the hole behind the stove for several more weeks. I had a bottle in which I could pee and a piece of wood on which I put my shit. Every day my parents placed food for me at the mouth of the hole and emptied the bottle and cleaned the piece of wood. My body ached all over and I stank.

But then the soldiers started to go from house to house searching for young men. It was lucky for us that they had no dogs. It was too dangerous for me then, so I went to join my brother and the others in the forest.

18 November 2006 (from my notebook):
We arrived back two days ago. Nanda in the shop, soft-skinned and smelling of Chanel Number 5. She is always so much smaller than I remember her.

I shone a torch into the water tank and there below the somnambulant goldfish was a pale-skinned frog, swaying with its arms lifted upwards, its eyes open and catching me in its gaze.

20 November 2006
Sunshine on my face and arms. The striped golden yellow on the mountainside opposite like woven silk. Two eagles flew just below our terrace so we could see the breadth of their backs and wings.

Last year the olives were plentiful, a great burst of black fruit covering the trees, and we went and bought four nets. Then the frost came and there was no point in picking them because the oil would be bitter. This year there are hardly any olives, but we have laid out our nets.

# The Priest's Diary

The priest started to write his diary when he heard the first rumours of war and, having started, he went on from one year to the next until just a few days before his death in 1966.

He used the back section of a big hardcover book in which he kept the

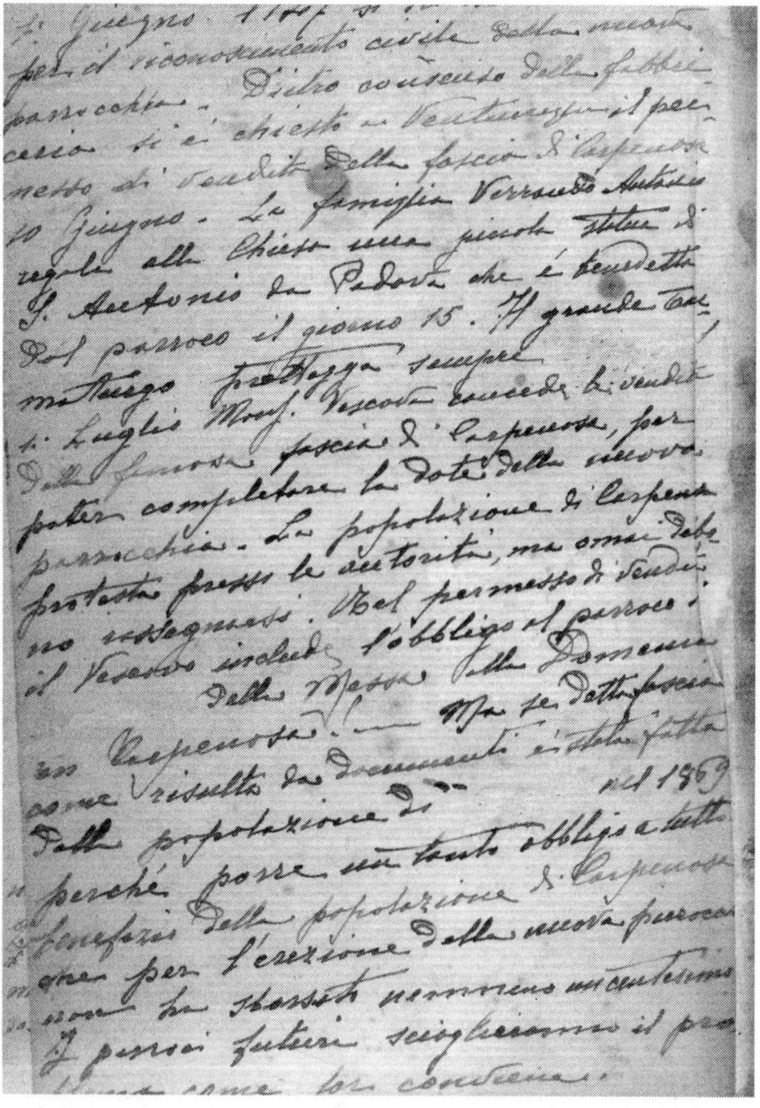

church accounts, his words crowding in right to the edge of each page. He wrote with a dip pen and produced wonderfully swirling capital letters. As the war progressed he began to write on small loose sheets of paper, which he must have sewn in later, or perhaps Pepina did it for him. I suppose he wanted to keep his commentary hidden from view in case it was found and used against him or others. Like all the priests, he knew too much about what was going on because he listened to confessions, but unlike some priests in other villages, he kept the secrets to himself.

The diary is peppered with lots of urgent underlinings and exclamation marks to give emphasis to the absence of food, the coldness of the weather and the gathering toll of unhappiness and violent death. When talking about who had been killed, the priest was careful to identify the person he spoke of with only a single initial, although some time after 1945 he went back to the text and added an asterisk and the full name in a little footnote.

Nella from the post office arranged for me to borrow the diary for a while. It is kept in a metal box in the church, but unlike the two brass candlesticks and the wooden crucifix whose Christ bore a strong resemblance to Giovanin the shepherd, no one has bothered to steal it.

Some of the pages are as fragile as dried leaves and the ink is very faded, but together with Eliana we managed slowly to untangle the old-fashioned script and to transfer it on to a computer. For three euros you can now buy a copy of the complete text in the local shop where it sits on the counter, propped up against the packets of dried figs and dates. There is a little photograph of the priest on the cover. He has a friendly, contented face and very big ears.

I have been reading the priest's account of the war. At Easter 1941, he says he received orders from his superiors that there would be no fasting for Lent and he clearly found this a ridiculous ruling, which showed a complete lack of awareness of the situation in a village like his, where, by then, people lacked most of the basic necessities of living and were already hungry all the time. By the autumn of the next year he writes that all they had to eat was a few potatoes, beans and chestnuts, and it was impossible to obtain leather to repair shoes.

'The people are complaining continuously and waiting for better times,' he says, adding rather ruefully, 'They address themselves to God with very little faith because they suppose that He is to blame for all their troubles.'

Over the next months he mentions the high cost of oil and flour, troubles with the chestnut harvest, the coldness of the winter and the ominous sight of English bombers passing overhead on their way back from attacking Genoa.

By the spring of 1943 the price of wheat reached thirty lire a kilo, by July the government had fallen and in September Italy was asking for an Armistice and the village was being invaded by 'straggling bands of poor soldiers trying to escape back to their own homes, begging for civilian clothes so as not to be recognised by the Germans'.

When Nella was reading this part of the diary she told me the story of a soldier from the village who was trying to get back here but was captured near the coast and put on a train bound for a camp in Germany. He said he remembered looking out through a window as the train passed by the mouth of the valley where the river joins the sea and this fleeting image upset him more than all the hardships that followed. Years later, when he was on the edge of dementia, he kept saying over and over again, 'I can see my home, but I can't get there! I can see my home, but I can't get off the train'. 'It was very sad,' says Nella, smiling as people often do when they are made shy by their own emotion.

In that same month of September 1943 the priest describes how 'The procession of the Madonna of the Rosary was forced to go along the path by the fields, because there were so many German vehicles parked on the road', adding, 'We now have here in Italy a German army, an English army, an American army, an Italian Fascist army and the army of the king, which is called the Badoglio army. The Germans are mining all the roads and bridges. Food has reached the highest prices. A single egg costs eight lire and shoes are twelve hundred a pair, if you can find them.

By February 1944 everyone is suffering because of the lack of salt and other necessities. On 18 March the village was preparing for another procession when two platoons of Fascist soldiers arrived, looking for deserters. They raided a number of houses and returned a few hours later with two young men, a few hunting rifles and a huge amount of cheese. They took the men, the rifles and the cheese away with them. This must have been the same occasion that Armando wrote about, when he and some others were stripped naked by the partisans down by the river.

# Blue Eyes

Adriana has been talking to her daughter Eliana about the priest's diary and it has woken old memories for her. 'We never like to speak of the things that happened during the war and maybe that makes it more of a burden for us,' she says.

She tells me about the German man who has bought a house just next to hers. He speaks only a few words of Italian but he smiles a lot and she likes him. But the other day he said *'kaput!'* and pointed to his car, and the word shocked her terribly and she had to hurry away because she was embarrassed at what he might think. 'It is not his fault,' she says apologetically.

Before we go to the kitchen, Adriana wants to show me a bit more of the house. She takes me into the room where the brother of the *padrone*, the man they called the Sea Captain, used to sit in silence for hours on end. He was shy and caused no trouble to anyone and he was always well-dressed and wore a hat, unlike the Engineer who was rude to everyone and wore the dirty working clothes of a peasant, and often went about with a wooden box on his back for collecting mushrooms in the forest.

The room is small and painted with flaking whitewash. It has a domed ceiling and a fireplace in one corner and a window with bars on it through which you can see some sheds and the tilt of the mountains. I try to imagine the Sea Captain sitting there in his fine clothes, staring at the logs burning in the grate.

The room smells sweet and musty, and there is a box of tiny shrivelled apples on the floor, next to a box of kiwis, one of onions and a sack of potatoes. The walls are festooned with mysterious objects. Adriana shows me a shallow metal dish with a folded lip at one side and explains that you put oil in the dish and lay a piece of plaited thread in it with one end hanging over the lip, and when you light it the room is illuminated by a tiny flame. 'You could just see who was there with you,' she says, 'and you could shell beans, but there was not enough light to read or to sew by.'

She shows me the metal containers that people used for transporting water. Her mother carried one like this strapped to her back when she and some other women walked to the coast to collect seawater, which could be boiled down and used as rough salt when there was none to be had during the last year of the war. Because of the soldiers, it was a very dangerous journey for the women to make, but they had no choice. 'Without salt you become ill,' says Adriana.

She shows me a bundle of thick leather goat collars with their bells still attached to them and a wire cage used for catching rats. She asks if I like kiwis and takes some from a cardboard box and puts them in a plastic bag; then we return to the kitchen.

We sit down, always in the same chairs and with the dog under the table. We each have a glass of the yellow wine that has just been bottled. Adriana starts to talk without me asking any questions.

She was eight when the Armistice was announced. Her father and her uncle Modesto were too old to fight and she had no brothers to be taken away, but she knew many of the young men who had gone to hide in the mountains. La Muta's two eldest sons were up there all the time. Arturo, her youngest son who couldn't move so fast because he'd had a limp ever since the accident, would go out at night and leave food for them. It was said he could walk in the dark like a cat.

A German general and a group of his soldiers took possession of the other half of Adriana's house, which meant that her aunt and her aunt's family had to move closer to the river, to the little house where Uncle Modesto lived with his wife.

The general was very ugly with a red face and a loud voice. He occupied the room next to the room where Adriana and her sister and mother and father ate and slept, while the soldiers were in the animal stalls down below. Her father was back home again by now and he provided them with food when they demanded it, even though there was not much to give.

At first the soldiers were nice to her. There was a man from Poland who was as tall as a tree; he could speak a bit of Italian and he said Adriana was like the daughter he had left behind in his own country. He said he only joined the war because otherwise his daughter and his wife were going to be shot and Adriana couldn't understand why anyone would want to shoot someone of her age. He hugged her once, that soldier, very tight, but she didn't mind because he was kind.

---

There was a fight. The partisans – for that was what they were all called now, even if they had no interest in politics but only in staying alive – attacked the Fascists close to the bridge not far from Adriana's house.

Adriana saw it happen. She was with the goats and her sister and an old man called Peppin who was good at laying the stones on mule tracks and was even smaller than her grandfather. First they saw some soldiers passing by, then there was the sound of gunfire. The goats scattered while the three of them hid behind a big chestnut tree; nobody bothered with them because they were too busy with each other. Peppin kept praying to the Virgin Mary to spare these little girls and promising all sorts of things in return. Then the fighting stopped. One of the Fascists was badly wounded and his friends made a rough stretcher and carried him away.

After that the general was very angry and Adriana would hear him shouting all the time, and even the Polish soldier stopped being friendly. The general sat on a chair outside the house smoking cigarettes and when Adriana had to walk past him he would say, '*Mama kaput! Papa kaput!*' drawing a finger across his throat in case she didn't understand what he meant. And he'd light a match and hold it close to the wall of the house and say, '*Casa kaput!*'

---

One day Adriana was coming down from the high pastures with her mother and sister and some other women. They were carrying big bundles of wheat-sheaves on their backs, tied up in lengths of cloth. As they were walking along the cobbled track close to the river a German lorry stopped and soldiers jumped out. They thought the women had been taking food to the young men in the mountains.

They thrust knives into the bundles and shouted, '*Dove banditi?*' They always referred to the partisans as bandits.

The women couldn't answer because they didn't know where the young men were hiding, but the soldiers were sure they were lying. They shook Adriana's mother by the shoulders as if to shake the words out of her, then one of them grabbed hold of Adriana. He led her to a big stone and pushed her down so that she was sitting on it. He took out his pistol and held it to her neck. '*Dove banditi?*' he said again, looking at the women, his finger on the trigger.

Adriana's mother was crying as she always did, but she was also telling her daughter to keep still, for God's sake to keep still. Adriana looked at her mother, amazed that an adult could do nothing to help her apart from offering a few words of advice. She looked up at the man with the gun, saw his cold blue eyes and understood that he would be capable of killing her.

She thinks she must have sat there for seven minutes at least before the soldier became bored with this little drama and put his gun away. Then all the soldiers wandered off with a few passing curses and the women gathered up their bundles of hay and went back to their houses.

⸻

There were more fights between the Fascists and the partisans, but the one that Adriana remembers most vividly was again close to the bridge. The partisans threw a grenade from the cliffs above and it exploded on the roof of her house, shattering the stone tiles. This was followed by a lot of gunfire and many people were killed from both sides. She saw dead bodies, she saw pieces of hair and skin.

That was when they went into hiding. They took what they could carry on their backs and followed the steep mule track to the village where her father had been born, then went further up into the chestnut forest until they came to a stone house hidden among the trees. About twenty others had arrived before them, including La Muta.

They stayed there for several weeks, living on chestnuts mostly, although sometimes Adriana's father or one of the other men was able to creep down at night to one of their abandoned houses and get some of the food they had hidden: flour in a demijohn bottle buried in a pit in the vegetable bed, potatoes from a hollow tree, dried beans in a sack in a hole in a terrace wall. When they returned the sack they always had to make sure to push back the roots of little plants so no one would notice the disturbance.

'But I wanted to tell you about that soldier,' says Adriana, 'the one who put a pistol to my throat. He came here, years later. There was a house for sale in this part of the village and a woman who spoke Italian arrived in a car. When she saw me she smiled and stepped forward to shake my hand. A man wearing a hat was sitting in the back of the car. "That is my father," said the woman. "He has a connection with the valley, from long ago."

'She made a sign to the man and he opened the car door and stepped out. He was old and bent, but still I could see that he was tall. He turned towards me and raised his hat like a gentleman.

'When I looked at his face I recognised his eyes and I knew at once who he was. I was shaking all over and I cried out with the shock.'

The man put on his hat, said something in German to his daughter and returned to the car. I never saw those people again.'

December 2006 (from my notebook):
A butterfly in the sunshine and leaves from the wisteria falling on my head. Now that all the churches in the valley have been robbed of the best of their treasures, locks have been put on their doors and alarm systems have been installed.

The Christmas Eve fire in front of the church: the red heart of the fire showing through the great boles of the tree trunks, like bodies burning on a pyre. Nella shows me what was not stolen from the church. The oldest Christ figure was in a cupboard hiding under all sorts of bits of cloth and she unwrapped his feet for me to see them. The priest's diary and other papers were safe in a chest, but one dark painting has been prised off the wall and another Christ was taken and the nails from the cross were left scattered on the floor.

# The Village of Terzina's Childhood

Armando says it was Old Tunin's son, Little Tunin, who was the hero of the Battle of the Bridge. The battle was organised by the leader they called Vitto and there were three bands of partisans, a total of around fifty men, and a great heap of Fascists down at the military base, maybe two hundred of them in all.

The attack took place under the cover of darkness and the partisans were perched like chamois in the steep and rocky landscape above the river. Tunin (I am dropping the diminutive from now on) threw a grenade that smashed the roof of the building where the commander was sleeping and it killed him outright. Then more grenades were thrown down and many of the Fascists were killed or injured.

'Tunin was like a fox, appearing and disappearing and firing from one place and then another, and the Fascists thought he was a dozen men,' says Armando.

Two or three partisans were wounded, but the Fascists were in chaos with several fatalities. They quickly collected their wounded and their dead, and got into their trucks and sped away, leaving a lot of food and ammunition behind them.

The partisans helped themselves to the weapons and celebrated what felt like a victory, but everyone was afraid of what might happen next. The people took whatever they could carry and went to hide in their huts in the chestnut forests. For a whole month or even longer everything was quiet and no one even spoke of the Fascists. It was as if the war was over.

But then the soldiers returned in their trucks and the reprisals began. In the village of the mills further upstream, they burnt people alive in their houses. In other villages they raped the women and killed the old people. They shot any young men they found. And the partisans stayed in their hiding places and watched it all from a distance and felt it was their fault because of the battle of the bridge.

---

I first met Tunin and his wife at the big family gathering which is held in honour of his father, high up on a mountain pass. He is eighty-seven, but you would never think it. He is small and wiry, the skin of his face stretched tight across the high cheekbones, with only a scattering of fine wrinkles. He races in his talk and in his movements, and I was told he races in his car as well and was currently waiting to hear if the police were going to take away his driving licence. His two passions are hunting for wild pig and hunting for mushrooms and he has his own mushroom patch up in the high mountains, and sometimes he spends the night sleeping on the ground beside his mushrooms for fear that someone might come and steal them. When he sings the old partisan songs, he has a strong high voice, which could almost belong to a young man.

His wife is called Terzina, 'the third one', because she was the third daughter born to her parents who were longing for a son. She is eighty-four

and also doesn't look it, except that her false teeth are bothering her and she moves them about a bit in her mouth. Her body is small and neat, and she has an elegant and somehow aristocratic face. She often wears black trousers and a little jacket.

When I introduce myself they both know about me from Adriana. Tunin clasps my hand in his dry hand and stares at me, smiling his wide smile. Terzina leans forward and takes my other hand.

'Come and see us and we will tell you stories that Adriana has not told you. We are in the house of my childhood, we are there every day at the moment. We see nobody because nobody passes by. Come!'

'How do we find you?' I ask.

'You shout and we shout back,' says Tunin.

---

And so on a summer's afternoon we walk to Terzina's village. We could have gone by car on a very steep and narrow little road, but it is nice to go along the path. Parts of it have broken away where a terrace has fallen across it and sometimes we have to clamber over broken trees, but the rest of the path is quite grand, with carefully paved steps on the steep bits and slabs of rock planted into the ground like gravestones to mark the way if you are following it in the dusk or by moonlight. We cross a bridge over a narrow stream, then zigzag up until we are under the village, the buildings towering like a muddled fortress above us.

We shout and there is an answering cry, and we go up steps that bring us out alongside a little church. In front of the church is a tiny stone square and beyond that there is a long table under a half-broken awning, and right

at the end of the table Tunin and Terzina are sitting side by side. Their shaggy puppy races towards us and dances a greeting.

'I didn't hear your car,' says Tunin, and when we say we came on foot, he laughs as if this is a wonderful joke. Terzina greets us more formally, getting up to be kissed on both cheeks before pointing at the little dishes on the table and telling us to eat. She has nuts and raisins and plums laid out and ready.

Tunin rushes off and reappears with a bottle of Martini and another of his own wine. He pours himself a Martini. Terzina has a black coffee and she tops it up with red wine. 'I always drink coffee this way,' she says.

I feel shy about asking them questions, but they both launch into stories about the past almost at once.

'I was hiding with the other young men in the woods above here, after the Battle of the Bridge,' says Tunin. 'It was winter and there was snow on the ground and we had nothing to eat.'

'You ate a cat!' says Terzina, shouting the information as if it makes her angry just to think of it.

'But we had no salt to cook it with!' Tunin shouts back and a look of disgust crosses his face as he remembers the taste of old roast cat.

'The women here had no food. All they had was chestnuts. They made a soup from chestnuts and took that to the young men who were hiding in the woods. The skin of their faces was covered in sores because of the chestnuts,' says Terzina and she puts her hand to her mouth because the sores look so painful. 'A month passed like that and then the Fascists came.'

Tunin waves his hand down to where the path we had followed enters the village. 'We watched them coming,' he says. 'We could have shot them, we could have killed them all, but then others would have come to punish and even to kill our wives and our mothers, our old people, our children. So we had to sit still. We could do nothing.

'But we got a message to a man who lived at the top of the village and when the soldiers were in earshot he shouted to them in a loud voice, "Ah, my masters, I have good wine for you!" and that served as a warning to everyone and gave them a little time.'

Terzina has been listening wide-eyed to her husband as if she has never heard the story before and now she repeats the words, 'Ah, my masters, I have good wine for you!' and with that she is back in the present moment of the long-ago past. 'There were some young men who had been eating chestnut soup from a big pan in the square and they ran away to hide when they heard those words,' she says, her voice suddenly urgent. 'But the women saw how they had left their footprints in the snow, so they took buckets of water and threw the water over the snow to make the footprints disappear.

'The soldiers entered the village. They had caught one of our young men. He must have been badly hidden. They pushed him against the wall of the church. We watched and didn't know what to do. One of the soldiers took hold of me and pulled me close to the young man and said, "Look, here is your fiancé, it is time to kiss him goodbye!" Of course he wasn't my fiancé, but I looked at him. They were asking him where the others were but he didn't answer; maybe he didn't know, because they had found him on his own.'

And now Terzina's voice is changing again as with slow steps she approaches the climax of her terrible story. 'The soldiers had their guns pointing at him and he knew he was going to be killed and there was nothing to be done. He lay down on the snow,' and with that this old lady suddenly makes the graceful gesture of a dancer, raising an arm above her head and stretching out one leg to show how the young man positioned himself on the ground. And she covers her face with her raised arm so as to not see the moment when the shot rang out and struck its target, then she and her husband look at the stone square in front of the church and watch with horror as the blood spreads out across the snow.

'So much blood,' says Terzina, her face anguished with the sight of it.

We drink wine and eat raisins and nuts and talk about hunting dogs now. When I want to go to the lavatory Terzina leads me into the house of her childhood, up the outside stairs to a little room crammed with a sea of beds, so that you can hardly thread your way past them. 'The family comes to sleep here sometimes,' she says, indicating the beds with a little sweep of her hand.

It is getting dark and Tunin and Terzina are leaving anyway, so they offer to drive us down to the village below. We climb into the car, but the puppy refuses to join us and races along the road ahead. Tunin drives like a maniac, looking for the dog, turning his head to talk to us in the back seat and shooting round the tight corners without even bothering to hoot his horn. God save all of us if anything had happened to come the other way.

.

12 January 2009 (from my notebook):
With the binoculars I watched a fluffed-up buzzard land on the thin oak tree just outside my window. He swivelled his head and shrugged his shoulders and swooped down to the slate bench. I saw a little scrabble of movement, then he was back on his branch with a protesting mouse under one clawed foot. He bent forward and pulled out a long red thread of mouse-life, then he lifted the little body up in his beak and tipped his head back and swallowed it whole, tail last.

# Terzina's Notebook

Tunin and Terzina live in an apartment in the town by the coast. They paid for the construction of the whole building in the 1960s and the other three apartments are occupied by their three children and their children's children in one interconnected family nest.

Tunin has been in hospital for a hip operation and he has been told he can't drive for a month, so he's stuck in the apartment and can't get back to the house of his childhood, or to his mushroom patch in the forest. Eliana told me that he was feeling very sorry for himself and might like to be visited.

I phone and speak to Terzina. 'I am the Englishwoman,' I say. 'We met in your village last summer.'

'Oh, I know you,' she says. 'Come and see us today if you can. We are here, always here, because of the operation.' I had forgotten how tentative and light her voice sounds, more like a young girl than a woman in her eighties.

Terzina explains how to find their apartment: it's next to the big roundabout, opposite the petrol station and above the funeral parlour. I ring the outside bell and her voice comes through a little speaker and the door clicks open. I go up the cold stairs, holding a metal railing. Here is Tunin waiting for me. He is leaning on crutches and he looks pale. 'Where is your husband?' he says almost angrily, peering down the stairwell for a second figure. He turns to Terzina who is now standing beside him. 'She has come without him! Why? Did he not want to see us?'

We go inside and I give them a little gift of some sheep's cheese from Nanda's shop. This makes him even more agitated. 'Is it that you think we have nothing, that you need to bring us food?' he says.

Terzina intervenes, hushing him and quieting his anxiety.

We are in the kitchen. From the long window I can see the pale spring sunshine and a thick line of traffic following the treadmill of the roundabout.

I sit down and Terzina offers me coffee. Tunin sits next to me and very gently takes my hand. He says he needs to get back to the valley because he is going mad in the town. 'I am in a cage,' he says and the tears are welling in his eyes.

'If he drives they will take away his licence for ever,' says Terzina over the spluttering of the coffee machine.

I tell him that yesterday we walked to the house on the crest of the mountains, where he and his family spent so many months during the summer.

'*Madonna!*' He smiles with excitement and his eyes go far away as if he were now approaching that house in the clear mountain air. 'Is the roof still on? Is the cherry tree still there? I planted it by the door, and when there was that storm Clelia and her sister hid inside and the lightning hit the trunk and burnt right into it, but the tree was not killed.

'We grew potatoes and wheat on the patch of land outside. You must have seen where we grew them! But maybe there is nothing left now.

'We were so tired, you cannot imagine how tired we were; then my

151

mother La Muta said, "We all need a rest, so let's go and fetch water from the spring!" The spring was far away, down from the saddle where the two paths divide. The women carried a big bucket on their head and the men carried a long pole with a bucket balanced at each end . . .' Tunin places one of his crutches on his shoulder to show how they did it.

He puts five spoonfuls of sugar into the cup of black coffee that Terzina sets before him and says that he was seventeen when he fell in love with her and she was fourteen. She looks at him across the table and nods her head.

He would take a little lantern and go at night from the mountain house down through the forest, then all the way across to her little village; a walk of three hours or more. He would hide behind a tree and wait until Terzina came outside to do a pee, and there was just enough time for them to kiss before she fled back.

One night he got lost in the moonless dark on his way home, so he settled himself to sleep among the spreading roots of a chestnut. Then there was the noise of footsteps and it was another boy who had been out courting just like himself, coming from a different village.

'But then the war came,' says Terzina, her voice suddenly severe.

'I do not want to speak of the war,' says Tunin and again he looks trapped and unhappy.

To change the subject I ask if they would like to come to our house for a meal, but this also upsets him. 'I am a *mezzadro*,' he says. 'Do you know what that means? It means we had nothing. It means the *padrone* not only took half, but took the best half of everything. I cannot come to your house to eat because I would feel inferior. I would feel that you were a *padrone*.'

He pauses and becomes quiet again, turning these thoughts over in his mind. Out of the silence he asks me if I believe in God. He says that even though he is not sure what he believes in, he cannot fall asleep if he hasn't crossed himself.

The talk moves back to the mountains. 'My mother walking up the path to the mountain with one child on a string and another in her belly and me beside her and a basket filled with bread on her head. We were *legati*,' he says, intertwining the fingers of his two hands together. 'And now we are lost! We were in paradise but we didn't know it and now I am in hell.'

'We have our children and our grandchildren,' says Terzina hopefully, 'and we have our old age.'

'I am in hell,' he repeats emphatically and the tears have returned to his eyes.

He points to a framed hunting licence on the wall. 'I love all animals. When I have killed a hare, it is so beautiful I would do anything to bring it back to life again.'

Before I go Terzina presents me with a notepad of loose pages. 'I thought to write about my memories,' she says, 'but I didn't get very far. Take it.'

'Come and see us again soon,' says Tunin. 'And make sure that you come with your husband next time.' I promise that I will.

That evening I settle down to read Terzina's story. It is a variation of what she told me before: the images that remain always vivid in her mind.

I was born on 7 January 1927. My parents were perfect parents. My childhood was happy and I would like to return to it . . . I stayed at school as far as the third grade, thanks to the sacrifices made by my family.

From the age of fourteen I was in love with Tunin and he was my only love and for better and for worse we have been married for sixty years. In my youth I had a hard time because of the war. Tunin was a partisan and I lived in fear and in the hope of being happy with him in the future.

Now I want to tell, if I can, of the day on which the German Fascists came to my village. It was January 1945. My father had gone with a sack of grain to the mill in the lower village. He took his identity card with him. It was about 11.30 and my mother was preparing the pasta we ate at midday – but on the next day the food was still on the table . . .

The Fascists arrived and they had surrounded our village and we found ourselves in hell. They were shooting from all sides. In our house my mother had cooked a pan of chestnuts for the partisans, the ones who were still in the village. There was about thirty centimetres of snow on the ground. The partisans who could escape had already disappeared but unfortunately three of them stayed behind and they were captured.

One of the captured men was already close to death when they found him and the others were caught in the snow at around two or three in the afternoon. They were brought to the square in front of the church.

I remember them well. The Commandant ordered them to raise their arms in a Fascist salute and to shout, 'Long live Il Duce!' I can never forget the dying one and how he lifted his arm and in such a feeble voice tried to shout, 'Long live Il Duce!'

I had to assist in the death of a partisan. The Fascists said they knew he was my fiancé and they asked if I wanted to kiss him goodbye and then they murdered him in front of me. I didn't want to look, but they pulled my hands away from my eyes as they shot him.

One of the partisans was murdered on the snow in front of the church. I remember how he lay down and put his hand over his face and bent his leg under his body, and I saw the bullet holes. Before they left the Fascists said they were coming back on the following day and we were not to touch the corpses. If they saw that we had, we would all be killed.

My father was returning to the village and when he heard the shots he was afraid of finding everyone dead. He crawled into a hole to hide until the shooting had stopped and then he continued on his way, leaning on a stick and breathing heavily so as to seem like a very old man. He found us all in the house, thankful to be alive.

My father didn't want to see the poor slaughtered bodies lying like that in the snow, so he and my uncle went to the priest in the next village and the priest agreed to let them bring the stiff bodies into the church.

The next day was a Sunday and early in the morning the Fascists returned. They accused my mother of giving food to the partisans and she did not deny this but said that she would have given food to them also, if they had asked her. The Fascists then ordered her to cook all the eggs we had in the house, the eggs which we kept like religious relics, and when she had cooked them they ate only the yolks and left the whites in the pan.

Of the captured partisans, two were killed before our eyes and one of the ones who was taken away was killed because he refused to betray his companions. He said, "You are all cowards!" and when he said that they shot him in the back. The fourth partisan did talk and that was how they knew all about us when they came back on the Sunday.

But they didn't kill us. I have much more to tell, but for now I stop here.

## 30 April 2010

The weather has been very moody. Yesterday afternoon the sky went dark, thunder shook through the valley and there were hailstones as well as rain. Then, as if a switch had been pulled, the sun came out, the birds were singing and everything green steamed with relief and you could almost hear the seeds in the ground stirring into life.

I am writing this sitting in the doorway of Carmo, Old Tunin's mountain house. We followed the path that starts underneath a swooping bend in the road just before you reach the pass.

'It's a broad path,' said Eliana when she was telling us how to find it, but its broadness has been much diminished until it's not more than a line, drawn as it were with an index finger, along the contour of the slope.

Blue sky and the utter clarity of the air now that the clouds have lifted. I look out at the bodies of the mountains all around me, their ribs and backbones and great sleeping limbs not yet covered by the foliage of larch and oak and chestnut. There is a scattering of oaks close by and I can see an orange and yellow tinge of colour in the tips of their branches where the leaves are on the edge of breaking through. Coming here we passed daffodils and tiny purple anemones, pushing up through the exhausted swathes of last year's grass.

The house is long and low. Most of it has fallen into ruin but one little independent room has been maintained by Old Tunin's family. There is a door that closes and a roof that must keep out most of the weather. A drawing of Old Tunin, printed on a plasticised board, has been fixed to the wall, along with his dates: 1898 to 1992.

One corner in the room has been used as a fireplace and dry branches and a few broken beams are piled up and ready for burning. There's a stump of wood that would serve as a stool. Three broken shards from an earthenware pot lie on the floor. The clay is surprisingly thin, with the mark of a soft thumbprint where the handles have been pressed into the round body of the pot.

I step outside the door and suddenly notice Arturo's name incised into one of the pale stones round the entrance. And the date: 18 August 1944. The worst part of the war is just about to begin, for him and for all the people in the valley, but he doesn't know that as he cuts the letters and numbers deep into the stone.

I sit in the breeze and the sunshine. The sea looks huge and wrinkled, and the horizon melts into the sky so that you can't see any division between the element of water and the element of the air.

A green woodpecker is making its dip-dip-dip cry and a few moments ago there was the mewing of an eagle although I couldn't see it anywhere. There have been no other signs or sounds of life at all, not even grass-hoppers or lizards because it is still too cold.

A lavender bush is to the left of the door and I think of La Muta pinching one of the flowers between her finger and thumb as she passes by and inhaling the sweet oily scent that enters her head with all the intensity of a sound. The remains of a broken umbrella lie like a dead bird next to the lavender, tufts of grass growing through the spokes and the torn cloth. The curved handle has been broken off, but I see it on the ground a few feet away, the metal ring that held the spokes in place winking softly as the light catches it.

The wind has picked up and it is noisy all around us.

# Ida and Armando

Now when he can't sleep at night Armando often writes about the past, but then in the morning he reads what he has written and burns it because it is too full of secrets.

He says he has written a lot about 'the bad people' from the village: the ones who joined the partisans just to betray their hiding places to the Fascists and the ones who were involved in the bloody vendettas that took place after the war was over. He writes down their names and what they did and how they were punished or avoided punishment, then he scrunches up the pages and sets light to them, watching his own words blacken and disintegrate. He says it might take three hundred years before the things he writes about can be spoken of, then he pauses to think it over and says maybe people will remain silent for ever because that is the only solution.

Armando and Ida both lost their partners in 2004; they died within a month of each other. After Ida's husband had been buried she got rid of Argo, the shaggy yellow hunting dog who could hardly walk any more, because she said that seeing him made her too sad. And she sold the minah bird in its cage to a pet shop owner, because it kept calling out her name in her husband's voice.

Every morning, even when it's raining or freezing cold, Ida walks down to the village and along the road as far as the cemetery with its jostling crowd of tombstones. She brings fresh flowers and stands for a while by the grave and looks at the lozenge-shaped photograph fixed to the slab of white marble. Then she walks back. Whenever she speaks of her husband and how he suffered at the end and how much she misses him, her eyes glisten with tears. He watches her from a photograph on the dresser in which his black hair shines like polished ebony and his lips have a red tint. Armando also misses his brother and the two of them often talk of him and how brave he was, how kind, how good, how handsome.

A widow and a widower, both in their eighties, they get on very well but they can never spend much time in each other's houses if no one else is there, because it wouldn't be right, a man and a woman alone together. I sometimes feel like a chaperone, keeping a careful eye on their friendship.

---

I went to see them today. Ida and I were in her kitchen when Armando appeared at the door holding a bottle of his own wine in one hand and a bundle of lined pages in the other, like a schoolboy with his homework. He sat down and started to go through the pages, checking that they were correctly numbered and in the right order. Then he gave them to me. 'It's not about the bad people,' he said. 'It's about my childhood.'

He is eager to talk. His words tumble out so fast that he keeps falling back into the local dialect and Ida has to make a translation for him. He tells me he was born in 1925 in a house above this one, which now belongs to a German couple called Schmidt. 'Mr Schmidt used to come and ask us questions, just like you do,' says Ida, 'but he never wrote anything down. He wanted to know what we ate and how we looked after the land and the names we give to things, but now he doesn't ask any more, I think he's too busy.'

Armando interrupts her. He explains that when he was eight months old and still wrapped in swaddling bands, there was not enough food to eat, so his mother took a job as a wet nurse for a family near the coast because that was a way of earning money and they needed a bit of money more than anything. It was decided that Pino, his elder brother, could remain at home to help his father, but Armando was handed over to his grandfather who lived in the next village, the one that can be reached by the Roman bridge.

His grandfather lived alone. He fed the baby on goat's milk, until he was ready to eat solid food. He cleaned him and swaddled him and when he was old enough to walk the two of them did everything together. Armando remained with his grandfather for the next six years and during that time he never saw his parents and never thought of them either, because he had forgotten their existence.

When he was finally brought back home he was frightened by the strangers who crowded around him. He says that was probably why he never really felt at ease with his mother or father; they always seemed very severe and distant. But his grandfather had come to live with them as well and had brought the two goats along, and that reassured him. And even though he was frightened of his parents, he loved his elder brother Pino from the first moment that he met him. Ida smiles when her husband is mentioned and turns round to the framed photograph, as if to make sure that he can hear what is being said about him.

————————————•————————————

One day – and it can't have been long after he came back to the village – Armando was sent up into the mountains with the sheep, but while he was watching a polecat the sheep disappeared.

He went looking for them and lost the path and it began to grow dark. He sat under some trees crying until he heard a voice calling for him and he saw Pino approaching with a lantern. Of course the sheep had all made their own way back and were safe in the stall.

He pauses to think a bit, then he says he is sure it was in this same year that two older boys, who didn't belong to the village but were the sons of a *padrone*, got hold of him and tied his penis very tightly to the frame of the bed in such a way that he couldn't untie it. Then they covered him with a blanket.

Ida remembers the boys. One of them had something wrong with him: his face was swollen and he was horribly cruel to animals, but no one could say anything because his father was powerful.

'That's him,' says Armando. 'A swollen face and he was very fat. So there I was screaming with pain but I didn't dare show my mother what was wrong and it was only when Pino arrived that I pulled back the blanket so he could see.'

'You were taken to hospital,' Ida tells him.

'I was,' says Armando and he squeezes his hands between his thighs and grimaces to show how much it hurt. For weeks afterwards they bathed his penis in a bucket of salty water until the swelling went down. 'My poor little prick!' he says, using the word *pizzolino*, which means 'little bean pod', and this makes Ida giggle like a young girl.

She wants to change the subject.

'I loved books, I could read a book in a single night and I did drawing and calligraphy,' she says. 'I would have liked to study Italian literature and history but I stopped going to school when I was nine. I was sent to learn sewing from the woman in the house near the cemetery. At night I ran home up the path from the river as fast as I could, because I was so frightened.

'My family was very poor,' she continues. 'My grandmother always wore a long grey skirt with deep pockets and when she saw us she would put her hand into a pocket and bring out a chestnut and give it to us as if it was a wonderful treat. Even for Christmas she gave us a chestnut.

'Oh, I wish I could remember more,' says Ida, 'but Pino was the storyteller and he never wrote things down like Armando does, and I am ashamed because I have forgotten everything. It's all gone!' and she throws her hands into the air as if she has made the past vanish with a conjuring trick.

With that she describes how Pino was caught up in the battle of Cassino, in a part of the country close to Rome, where the entire town was bombed so heavily by the Allies that it was turned into a heap of rubble with not a single building left standing.

'Pino hid in a haystack,' Ida says, 'and there was a young girl of his age hiding there as well. He told me, "I grew my first moustache that night." He always wanted to find out if the girl was still alive, he wanted to see her again.' She giggles some more with the uncertainty of quite what her husband meant by this.

15 April 2010 (from my notebook):
A big green lizard has emerged from its lair in the wall by our front door. I heard it blundering about and caught sight of an absurdly bright flash of colour. No toads as yet. No planting of tomatoes as yet, but I have got three sacks of donkey manure. The climbing plant with pendulous orange flowers, which Agostina of the Little Thrushes gave to me, has survived the winter and now it has the first stirrings of red buds. I think of Agostina whenever I pass it and I wonder how she is. She and her husband are somewhere in a little apartment in the town, but I can't find their address.

21 April 2010
The female toad has arrived. She is even bigger than I remember her and she spends many hours of each day sitting immobile on the edge of the higher tank, staring at nothing in particular with her fox-red eyes. I watch her with the binoculars, so as not to frighten her.

26 April 2010
Three toads: the very large female, a less large female and a tiny male.

27 April 2010

The lower tank is festooned with the long threads of toad spawn. It's drawn in loops round the stalks of the water-lily and it scribbles a hieroglyph across the grassy green weed. The frog tadpoles swim around it. The large toad had her head just out of the water and watching her with the binoculars I realised that her diminutive husband was perched on her head like a bonnet.

# Partisans and Then House-Guests

Now Armando has had enough of listening to Ida and he is eager to take over. He talks about when he and Pino were with the partisans in the mountains. One day Pino said he was tired of living like a fox in a hole, so he walked back down to their home in the village in broad daylight. He was carrying a rifle and a pistol, with a belt of cartridges round his waist and two hand grenades in his pockets. He dumped them all on the kitchen table as if they were a load of vegetables and at that moment someone further down the valley whistled three notes to warn them that the Germans were approaching. Pino and Armando were told to crawl into the gap behind the stove, while their mother bundled all the armaments into the oven, which hadn't been lit, although it was still warm from the previous night.

Their father was always very nervous. He drank a glass of wine to stop himself from shaking because he was sure the grenades were about to explode and all would be lost. Their mother was much more practical and now she put the dough for a new loaf of bread to rise in the front of the oven, just as the Germans hammered on the door and walked in. They searched the house, but all they found was some dried pasta and some olive oil, which they took with them when they left.

'But we were lucky here,' says Armando. 'in all those months we only lost three young men from this village, the ones who were found hiding in a cave. Everyone else survived. The people further up the valley suffered

162

much more. Our women and girls were not raped, our houses were not set on fire – or at least they were, but not with people locked inside.'

'Oh, but we were so afraid of the German Fascists!' says Ida. 'I remember that day in February 1944. My father and two other men were coming down from the high pastures with hay on their backs and they saw a line of soldiers on the mountain road so they went to warn the partisans. But one of the partisans was a spy and he told the Fascists of the betrayal.'

More than a hundred men were made to assemble in the church square and the spy walked slowly among them, examining their faces. He pointed at Ida's father and at the other two, and they were brought out from the group and had their feet bound and their hands tied behind their backs with wire. They were propped up in a line, leaning against the church wall like sacks of chestnuts, and left there all night with a soldier guarding them.

Agostina's father was captured with Ida's father and Agostina remembers going to the church square in the morning. She says her father's wrists were so swollen she couldn't see the wire that bound them. She cried out and dived under the legs of the soldiers to try to reach him, but she was pulled back.

The priest was there too, pleading for the lives of the men. He said they all had families and he pointed at Agostina weeping in her mother's arms. He said he was quite sure there were no partisans in the chestnut forest, they were far, far away. 'If we find partisans we shoot these three, if not we let them go,' said the Fascists.

They left their prisoners and went to the highest part of the village with their guns. For what seemed like a long time there was the sound of shooting as they raked the trees with bullets. All the people watched in stunned silence because they knew the partisans must be hiding in stone huts and in hollow trees. When there was no movement among the trees, no sudden cry of pain from a bullet finding its mark, Ida's father and Agostina's father and the other man were set free.

That same night a group of German soldiers turned up at Ida's house. They brought some candles they had just stolen from the church and they were full of talk and laughter and said they wanted to eat a fine meal.

'My mother was a very good cook and they knew that,' says Ida.

'She was also very beautiful,' says Armando rather ominously. 'They knew that as well.'

Ida ignores him. The German soldiers wanted to eat, so her father killed their last rabbit and a baby goat and fetched the vegetables he had been preserving so carefully, and her mother began to prepare a feast.

While they were waiting the German soldiers went to search the house next door for partisans. They found a big pile of potatoes in the downstairs storeroom and they jabbed their bayonets in among them. There were two young men hiding under the potatoes but the bayonets didn't go deep enough. The young men kept silent and still, so they survived.

There were other young men hiding quite close by in the forest. When they smelt the food cooking they thought the Germans must have gone. They approached the house and threw pebbles against the window to say that they were hungry too. Ida's mother had to go out into the night to warn them of the danger. She made a sound like the hooting of an owl and they understood.

'Hoohooo!' says Armando, imitating the cry of the Eagle owl, which still makes its home in this part of the valley.

———————————•———————————

The talk of war has finished and Ida is telling me that she met Pino in 1945 when she was nineteen and as soon as they had married they went to live in a new apartment block on the coast and he had a good job in the building trade. They became friends with a much older married couple who lived in the flat below theirs and when Pino announced that he was retiring and he and Ida were returning to the village of their childhood, this couple asked if they could come and visit them, perhaps they could stay for a week or two?

So it was agreed and they arrived with their suitcases. They were given the bedroom next to the kitchen and there they stayed from one week to the next. They were both in their seventies but they were in good health. The old man was a house guest for ten years, while his wife reached the age of a hundred and one. 'She was part of the family,' says Ida. 'We did everything together.'

Ida's mother came to live with them as well, but just for a few months.

Her husband had died suddenly one night during a rainstorm, but in spite of the loss she remained fiercely independent and wanted to stay where she was. But then one day Ida found her lying on the ground after a stroke, so she couldn't be left alone any longer.

She was very angry about this change of circumstance and kept demanding to be returned home. She wouldn't eat anything and only drank water or *acquacotta*, so as a result she became very thin and frail.

But then one evening Ida made a big pot of soup, with meat in it as well as vegetables. The five of them sat round the table – the two old people were still there as house guests – and Ida's mother had a second helping and a third.

'I had never seen her eat so much and as she ate the colour came back to her cheeks, her eyes grew wide and sparkled and she looked twenty years younger. It was like a miracle. We stared at her in amazement.'

On the following day, as Ida was helping her mother to put on her knickers, she let out a little sigh and fell dead into her daughter's arms. 'She fell so softly,' says Ida almost in a whisper, as she holds the slight weight of her mother in her thoughts.

'I remember,' says Armando. 'Pino came to find me, to tell me what had happened.'

'She had been a very beautiful woman,' says Ida, 'and she did look lovely even after she had died.'

Armando agrees: 'She was famous for her golden hair.'

# People Talking

I suppose I have always felt more at ease living in a foreign country where my background and history are not relevant because they belong to a different world.

Here in the valley I am a foreign woman married to a foreign man, but people like the fact that we are here for much of the year and have chosen to live in a remote house that was empty for a long time.

In the spring I make jam from the thick-skinned lemons and in the summer I make jam from the fruit of the two apricot trees I planted with their roots in the soft ashes of my almost daughter whose hair in the sunlight was the colour of apricots.

In the early winter we discuss the state of the ripening olives on our trees with friends and neighbours, and try to decide on the right moment for harvesting. When the decision has been made the two of us struggle with ladders and long sticks, and rattle the fruit into the nets we have laid out for them, and pick away the broken leaves and twigs and put them in hessian sacks and take them to the only local press that doesn't mind dealing with such very small quantities. Two years ago we produced twelve litres of our own thick and peppery yellow-green oil and with that we felt like magicians who had accomplished the trick of a lifetime.

This winter has been very hard. People say that the last time they can remember it as bad was in 1947. 'The winter of my conception,' I say, by way of conversation.

I do sometimes talk about my past life, little snippets of information that seem relevant at one moment or another. When Agostina tells me about the death of her father I tell her that my father died at the same age, but with no thrushes in his waistcoat pocket. She looks at me sideways and nods her head as if she had known that all along. I tell Adriana that, like her, I also learnt to love my mother in the end, and Adriana says she is glad about that because it's the end that matters most. And when I see Armando busy with his chickens and rabbits and with the noisy donkey called Garibaldi and the goats that keep escaping I tell him that I used to live on a farm where we had pigs and sheep and chickens, and my daughter even brought up two fox cubs. He grins at the thought, although I am not sure if he believes that there really are foxes and pigs and chickens in some other place far from this one.

# Armando Sees the World

When I got back home that afternoon I read the story Armando has given me. He has filled seven pages with his careful script and there is not a word about the bad people who are so often in his thoughts and nothing about the war either.

In the opening line he writes, 'What I am going to tell you is not only my story, but the story shared by many young people who were just like me. We all wanted to find a better life and so we all wanted to move away from the village, to live in a city and to find paradise there.'

Armando was ten years old. He had finished his schooling and it was the month of June when a childhood friend of his father's came to visit. This man was called Gigi and he had left the valley and had set up his own flower-growing business on the coast at San Remo. Things were going very well and he had more than sixty thousand carnations growing in his fields; that was why he wanted to employ a young boy to work for him. Armando listened to Gigi talking and said at once that he would like to take the job. His parents protested and said they didn't want him to go, but he had made up his mind.

They had no suitcase in the house, so his mother packed a spare pair of trousers and a second shirt and a straw hat into a jute sack. Armando was so excited about the idea of going to a city: 'it was like touching the sky with the tip of my finger.' He lay awake all that night, thinking about his new life and listening to the blackbird singing in the tree just under his window.

Gigi arrived to collect him in the morning and even carried his sack for him as they walked down to the main street in the village. Here was Gigi's bright red Guzzi motorbike, a two-seater with a little carrying box just big enough to hold the sack.

Many people from the village had gathered to watch Armando leave. He climbed up on to the seat behind his new master and held on to him round the waist. People waved goodbye and the machine went pop-pop-pop and off they flew in a cloud of smoke and dust.

Are you all right there? asked Gigi, but Armando was too terrified to speak.

They reached the coast. He saw the blue expanse of the sea for the first time in his life and he saw two tiny boats dancing on the water. Gigi said, 'They have been out fishing and now they are coming back!'

Then he saw the railway line and the noisy long serpent of a train moving along it and still he was so afraid he couldn't speak.

They took a turn to the right up a steep hill and they arrived at a house. 'Theresa, come and see this boy I have brought for you,' said Gigi, calling out to his wife.

Theresa was very friendly. 'What is your name?' she asked. 'You look a little pale. Don't you feel well?' but Armando remained silent.

So his new life began. Everyone was very kind. He learnt how to cut the carnations and to do all the other tasks that were set for him. He ate well, the work was not as hard as the work at home, there was electric light, which he had never seen before, he could watch the train and he could look at the sea.

But as the months passed he began to miss the blackbird who used to sing in the nut tree outside his window. He missed the sound of the river and he missed his own poor house and the goats in the shed and his brother and sister and most of all his grandfather who had cared for him for so many years. His grandfather had once told him, 'If you want to be happy, you must never leave your own village' and now he understood the truth of these words.

Theresa saw that he was sad. She asked him to sit beside her. 'What is the problem?' she said. 'Are we working you too hard? Do you not feel well?'

'No,' said Armando, 'everything is fine. It's just that I want to see my home again.'

'You will have ten days at home for Christmas,' she said and she embraced him like a mother.

So on 23 December 1936 Armando was getting ready to return to his village. Before leaving Theresa gave him a pair of new shoes, a new shirt, everything. And when he was dressed she took him to stand in front of a full-length mirror; he didn't recognise himself and thought he must be looking at a doctor's son.

Gigi gave him a box of mandarins and some little cakes and because he had worked for six months he was given a bonus of 180 lire, in ten-lire notes, with an extra twenty lire as a Christmas present. All three of them climbed on to the motorbike and as he left Armando thought, 'This is the last time I shall see the sea,' but he kept this knowledge as a secret in his heart.

His mother embraced him when he arrived and marvelled at how much he had grown. He carried the box of mandarins and cakes into the house and he was so pleased to see his grandfather that he didn't even think of saying goodbye to Theresa and Gigi.

It took him a while before he dared to tell his family that he was never going back to the coast.

'That is how we mountain people are,' he writes in his rolling script. 'We are attached to our own soil, our own way of life. Many of us went away like I did in search of a better life, but having tried it, we returned home.'

Armando has remained in the village ever since. He married a local woman and brought up two pretty daughters. Because he and his family were poor they lived in part of the priest's house next to the church. That was how he got to know Pepina so well and how he knew that she and the priest slept in the same bed together, no matter what anyone said to the contrary.

For many years he worked as an inspector of the hunt, a job that obliged him to walk all the paths in the mountains and to look around him. He was not popular because he was far too keen on imposing fines and would even lie in wait for hunters who he suspected might be killing things they were not supposed to kill. When first his mother and then his father died, he returned to the house of his childhood. He kept a tame fox for a while and at one time he had seventy wild pigs in the sheds that had been used for cattle.

He went hunting with Tunin and the other men who knew each other from the partisan days. Even now he still goes hunting for the wild pigs in the autumn, wearing an army camouflage jacket and carrying his old rifle and grinning with excitement. And in the months of January and February he takes a different gun and goes to hunt little birds. He shoots as many thrushes as he can find, but he says he always spares the blackbirds because they sing so prettily.

# Saint Francis and the Birds

Armando still keeps two or more thrushes in cages outside the sheds where he has his rabbits and chickens and sheep. During the very cold weather they are brought inside and when it is very hot he covers the barred roofs of their prisons with bunches of leaves to give them shade. I sometimes think of releasing them, coming under the cover of darkness like the partisans who knocked on the door of the barn where Armando and his companions were sleeping. A few urgent words of exhortation and then a flutter of wings and they would be out in the night air and maybe so confused that Armando would catch them first thing in the morning.

January and February are the months allocated for the hunting of songbirds. Sometimes a solitary hunter will park his car halfway along our track, which doesn't belong to us until the very last stretch, then you hear the sound of gunshots. There is nothing we can do to stop them, but we did buy a little figure of Saint Francis with three white birds settling on his hands and a halo on his head and we have made a little shrine for him in a terrace wall close to the place where the hunters turn their cars round. Maybe it makes them pause for a moment.

Certainly the songbirds have no faith in human beings. I have tried hanging strings of peanuts or fatballs in the trees close to our house, but the food is left untouched. If a robin or any other small bird catches sight of you they have a way of diving out of sight that I have never seen them do in England. For a while in England there was a robin that used to fly into my kitchen and stand on the table eating crumbs; once it even fed from my hand. I told Armando about it, but he clearly didn't believe me.

# Tunin and the Scent of Lavender

14 April 2010 and this time I go to visit Tunin and Terzina with my husband, as promised.

Tunin is delighted. He stands in the doorway to welcome us and he holds Herman's hand and gazes into his face and strokes him on the shoulder. I have never met such an eagerly tactile man who wants to know everything through the sensation of touch. His behaviour is not incongruous or disconcerting, it is as much part of his character now as it must have been when he was a child.

'Sit here, next to me,' says Tunin and he pulls his chair very close to Herman. 'You fell in your car, just like I did,' he says and I realise that this is one of the bonds of closeness that he feels, the shared experience of falling and not knowing if you will be alive when you reach the ground. 'Were you hurt?' he asks tenderly. 'Did you get wounded here?' He leans across and his fingers lightly touch the long scar on Herman's neck, which is where he was operated on during the cancer treatment.

Terzina has made coffee and we pause in this talk of accidents to drink it. Terzina looks at her watch and says she has to go and collect one of her grandchildren. When she has gone I ask Tunin about being a partisan during the war. I suppose I think he might feel freer to talk.

'I cannot speak of it!' he says emphatically. 'There are people who are still alive, or their children are still alive, and that is why I cannot speak of it. It would cause trouble.

'I was twenty when I was conscripted into the army,' he says, the words

171

tumbling after each other. 'I put formic acid in my left ear, pushed it in with a stick, because I didn't want to be sent to die in Russia. I was riding my bicycle when the eardrum burst with a bang.' He bangs his fist on the table to illustrate the sound. 'The doctor who saw me was a good friend and he told the authorities it was an old trouble.

'So I was not sent to Russia and I became a sort of manservant to three officers in the town. I did all the cooking and shopping and cleaning for them and one of the officers had a very nice wife who was at home a lot of the time. One day when I came in, her husband was sitting at the table and loading his pistol. He looked at me very carefully, holding the pistol towards me, and it was to tell me to stay away from his wife, although it wasn't necessary because I was engaged to my Terzina and I visited her every Sunday, so I didn't need to make trouble with other women.

'Then came September 1943.' Tunin sucks in his breath with the thought of that date and all the changes it brought to his country. 'No king and no government and the German Fascists as well as our own. I went back to my village and two Slavonian partisans arrived at our house late one night. They told us we must join them in the fight and they had rifles with the

hammer and sickle stamped on the wood. That impressed me. I became a partisan. I signed up.

'I won't talk about the terrible things that I saw,' says Tunin and you can see that the terrible things are passing before his eyes as he speaks. 'Three times I saw men being killed and I could do nothing about it . . . I was in the mountains with some others and we captured ten Italian Fascists and three German soldiers. They had more weapons between the twelve of them than we had for fifty men and we took their weapons without killing anyone. I confronted a German soldier and he put his hand to his pistol, but I was too quick for him. I took his hand grenade, but I dropped it later in the day and that was a disaster.

'We had all those Fascists tied up as our prisoners and that was when I noticed that they smelt of lavender, even their weapons smelt of lavender. Only later I learnt they had just come from my house where we had been making lavender oil. They had burnt my house to the ground, everything gone, the lavender, our animals, all our food.

'You know what lavender is?' asks Tunin as if he is waking from a trance. 'The flowers, the blue flowers . . .

'The hunger,' he says, still racing through the past. 'I had only a pocket full of raw chestnuts and the other men wanted to share them with me because they had nothing.'

Terzina has come back with her grandchild, an elegant young boy wearing spectacles who greets us with the friendly disdain of a city dweller. The spell is broken. Tunin offers his grandson a biscuit and when the offer is cheerfully rejected he mutters about hunger and nobody these days knowing what it means. He says he doesn't want to speak any more because of the spies and all the troubles that came after the war and when I ask him if he fought alongside the writer Italo Calvino he says he did, but he doesn't want to speak of him either because the things he wrote down later about the partisans were all lies.

---

We change the subject. In 1947 Tunin and Terzina were married and they opened the shop – the same shop that Nanda now owns. They would go on foot with haversacks on their backs, collecting the food they were going to sell. Tunin says he once carried three hundred eggs on his back and another time he carried a sack of bran that weighted fifty kilos all the way down from a high village on the other side of the valley. He did it for a woman whose husband had been killed by the Fascists, so she was on her own and needed help.

It's time for us to go. Tunin gets to his feet without using the crutches and embraces both of us and says he wants to see us again soon. Terzina says that while he is not allowed to drive, she plays cards with him every night, because it's the only way to keep him from getting too depressed.

Tunin listens to her and nods his head. 'Maybe I will die soon,' he says, 'now that there is nothing to live for.'

'What can we give them?' Terzina asks him as if she hasn't heard him correctly. She tips the rest of a packet of chocolate wafers into a plastic bag and hands that to me.

# Strangers in a Strange Land

Talking to Tunin I realised that for him the modern town that has been his home since 1953 is a foreign country. He is still an outsider, an immigrant without the roots of belonging.

Many years ago when I was in Australia working on a book I met an old man from the Pitjantjanjara tribe. He had grown up among the red sands of the Nullabore Plain in the vastness of the Great Western Desert but was now confined to a state-run Aboriginal reserve that had been set up near the coast.

The reserve was like a little township, with geometrically planned roads and neat lines of houses, but the people refused to live in them and they had set up their own ramshackle campsites made out of corrugated iron and bits of stick and cloth and plastic.

'We are strangers here,' said the old man, his eyes blank with despair. 'The sand here is the wrong colour,' and he picked up a handful of grey dust and let the alien substance trickle through his fingers.

---

Tunin sits in the kitchen of the apartment block he paid for with his own money and stares out of the window with an expression of baffled dismay at the roundabout with its steady rumble of traffic. 'The wind here is different from the wind on the mountains,' he says. 'I am trapped in a cage.'

There is a huge sense of nostalgia for the land he has lost, as if it were several thousand miles away instead of an hour's car drive, but his home is lost in time as well as in space. The door is shut.

'Take me there, take me to the mountain, take me to Carmo where we spent so many summers. I would like to sleep under the stars,' he says, a child's pleading look on his face.

Terzina watches him and keeps silent. She is willing to go with him to the houses of their birth, to tend the vines and prune the olives and grow a few beans and check up on the dogs that are looked after by other people when they are away, but she has always refused to spend even a single night there. If they did that, Tunin would never agree to return with her to town.

# Adriana Meets the Woman in White

Adriana stopped going to school in 1946. She had just turned eleven and was needed at home. She says the war had made her silent and fearful, and even after it was over and the Americans had dropped cigarettes and chocolate from the sky, she could not forget the dead men she had seen lying on the ground, their hair, their skin. And she couldn't forget the soldier who had held a gun to her throat and the knowledge that he was prepared to kill her, even though she was just a child and a stranger to him.

She was very thin and frail and she was often ill and had trouble with breathing, and the pains in her back became so bad that she had to be taken to hospital where they made a photograph of the bones and suggested some heat treatment her parents could never afford.

'Many of us were like that,' she says. 'We moved in a dream, because of what had happened, what we had seen. And then in the months after the war there were people hanged or shot or seeming to have taken their own lives and nobody wanted to ask any questions. I can't talk about it,' says Adriana. 'Even now it makes my heart race.'

She sits there in her kitchen, her eyes briefly filled with fear. 'Patience,' she says and the mood is lifted.

'When I had just turned fourteen,' she says, 'I understood things I had not understood before.'

'What sort of things?' I ask.

'At home I had no freedom. I had to ask permission for everything. I even had to ask permission if I wanted to spend a few minutes playing with stones by the river. My mother was always angry with me, telling me I should have been born a boy. But then I discovered that life could be different.'

---

She was by the river with her father and she saw La Muta's son Arturo working with his father in a little field of flowers on the other side of the water. Arturo was nine years older than her and she thought he was a beautiful young man. She saw that he had a limp, but she knew nothing about the accident to his knee, which had left him with one leg much shorter than the other. She assumed he had hurt himself just recently.

But what she noticed most keenly was the way Arturo and his father behaved together. She saw Old Tunin taking his son's hand to steady him and she saw how close the two of them were and how they loved each other, easily and with confidence.

As she watched the tenderness between them, she felt pity for Arturo because his leg was hurting him so much – and the pity was like falling in love, even though she didn't realise it at the time.

Not long afterwards she heard that Arturo was ill in bed with a fever.

She went with her mother to visit him, walking the path up from the river to the house among the olive groves called the House of the Warm Spring.

They found La Muta sitting beside her son who was lying on a bed of hay and although Adriana was shy and had nothing to say, she felt closer to this family than she had ever felt to her own. She felt she belonged with them. And she felt as if her life was balanced on the edge of something.

'And then I met the Englishwoman,' she says and tells me this story.

She was on her own with her goats down by the river. They had five goats and the bells on the collars round their necks all clanked with a different note as they moved their heads so she knew each one by the sound it made.

She remembers that the sun was shining and she was sitting with her back against the big chestnut tree, the one that she and her sister and the old man called Peppin had hidden behind when there was a fight between the partisans and the Fascists.

She heard a low rumbling noise and looked up to see a car creeping along the track that followed the bends of the river. During the war a lot of military trucks and jeeps had passed this way, but since then there was hardly any motor traffic apart from the rickety bus that went up the valley in the morning and down again in the evening and her uncle Modesto's battered Fiat 413, which he used to collect the milk from different parts of the valley.

The car that approached her now was like nothing she had seen before. It was black and shiny and huge. 'I'll find the photographs,' says Adriana, 'and then you'll see what I mean.'

The car came to a stop and a man stepped out. Adriana is very clear about his appearance. He was wearing a pale straw hat and a dark jacket and a white shirt and white trousers with a sharp crease in them and he had a yellow silk cravat tied round his neck. He was cleanshaven and he looked so confident and wealthy that she thought he must be an important Fascist who knew this place and had returned to look at it again.

The man opened the rear door of the car and a fine lady stepped out like a figure from a fairy tale. First a white shoe with a little heel and a

buckled strap, then legs encased in shiny stockings, a white skirt that covered big thighs and reached down to her calves, a belted white jacket, a white scarf and long white gloves. Adriana had never seen gloves before and she stared at them in amazement.

The lady's hair was a silvery colour and it was piled on to the top of her head in a heap of little curls. She was carrying a black handbag and a black walking stick.

She took a few steps towards Adriana, leaning on the stick. 'Don't be afraid!' she said in Italian, her voice very slow and deep, and even though

Adriana could understand her words it sounded as if she was speaking a language she had never heard before.

'Don't be afraid, I am not a wolf, I am not going to eat you!'

'I told her I was not afraid,' says Adriana, 'even though this wasn't true. And I called the goats to me as if they could protect me.' And with that she makes the little kissing sound that would bring the goats closer and she grins at me because she is very much enjoying the telling of this story.

The lady told Adriana that she was English and she had a villa in San Remo. She said she knew the valley from long ago and she was friends with the family who owned much of the land by the river.

I ask Adriana what the lady was called, but she cannot remember. 'She had a white fishing net with her,' she says, 'the kind they use for catching butterflies. But I think he was carrying the net for her. I think he was her husband but I am not sure. He was very polite to her and he always held her arm when she walked.'

The lady asked if Adriana would mind having a photograph taken and the man with the cravat brought out his camera and the lady settled herself on the grass like a broody hen. Adriana sat behind her and stroked one of her goats. She had never been photographed before. The man took another photograph of Adriana on her own, just as she was calling all the goats to her and she didn't like that because he hadn't asked her first.

The lady said she would make copies of the photographs when they had been printed and she said she would like to come to Adriana's house to meet her family.

So they set off along the track, Adriana carrying a bundle of broom on her head and the goats milling around her while the strange beast of the car followed until they reached the huddle of buildings close to the river where she lived with her sister and her parents and her aunt and her children and Uncle Modesto and his wife and her mother's parents and Peppin who had never married.

Adriana thinks the man stayed in the car, but she is not sure. She remembers the lady dressed in white coming down the steps to the terrace in front of the dark stalls where they kept the animals and the casks of wine and the tools for the land. She remembers her sister sitting outside an open door stripping the papery leaves from the maize and she looked up briefly but said nothing, which was always her way of dealing with shyness. She remembers her mother appearing and being angry because she didn't know who this strange woman might be and assumed that she was here because Adriana had done something wrong.

Then Grandfather Avostin arrived. He always wore a big cloth cap on his head to make himself look taller, but still he was tiny and only reached Adriana's shoulder when he stood beside her. People called him Avostin of the Mill because he had once worked in a mill, but that was long ago and now he was well into his eighties and kept himself busy with beekeeping and winemaking and the pursuit of women. He often set off on foot to the nearest town in the valley, saying that he was going to look for a woman. Adriana liked him very much. She even liked him when he was drunk, because then he behaved like a child who was even younger than she was.

Avostin was not afraid of strangers and he stood in front of the lady, his eyes on a level with her bosom. He tilted his face up towards her.

'Who is this?' he asked Adriana.

'I met her by the river.'

'Does she want wine?'

The lady said no, but she would like a glass of water.

Adriana fetched water for her in a tin mug and she remembers how she suddenly felt ashamed of the thin faded cotton of her skirt and blouse, the cloth slippers on her feet. She felt ashamed because she had never been to a big town, so she didn't know what a villa might look like. She had never even seen the sea except as a glimmering triangle in the far distance.

And as she thinks back on this meeting she realises that the man with the cravat must have been there as well and not in the car, because he took a photograph of old Avostin in the shadow of a kiwi plant with his hands above his head and a little cloth bag round his shoulder, and another in which Adriana's mother and her aunt's youngest son stand next to him, while Adriana and her sister were told to balance themselves on chairs behind them so that they could all be in the picture together. When they got the photograph they found their heads had been cut off.

After a while the lady was ready to leave and she asked Adriana to

accompany her to the car. That was when she said, 'I feel as if I know you already. I was thinking that perhaps you would like to come with me to England. You could continue your studies at school. I would look after you as if you were my daughter.'

Without stopping to think for even a moment Adriana said yes, she would like to go to England. She would like that very much.

'It's true,' says Adriana now, 'and I should have gone. I have often wished that I had. My life would have been very different, wouldn't it?'

'So why didn't you go?' I ask her.

Adriana looks apologetic. 'If the lady had come a bit later, maybe just three months later, I would have been stronger and I would have been able to defy my mother. But I still felt so helpless.

'My father said I could do as I wished, but my mother cried and screamed and ran around the house and said it would break her heart, I was too young, I would be ruined, terrible things would happen to me. I couldn't resist her.'

The lady came to the house a couple more times. On the final occasion Adriana's hair had been cut into a bob just below the line of her jaw and she was wearing a pretty dress with flowers on it. The lady's companion took a photograph of her standing with one hand resting on the shiny black

body of the car, while her sister and her parents stand in a line behind her. In the photograph she appears very grown up and sophisticated and not at all like a fifteen-year-old village girl who knows nothing of the world. There is a look on her face that combines longing with nostalgia, as if she has persuaded herself that she really is about to leave for ever and she knows she will miss her home and that she will never return to it.

But then the lady said goodbye to old Avostin and to all the family and she kissed Adriana on both cheeks. And that was that. Her companion opened the car door for her and he sat himself in the driving seat and the car grumbled to life and she waved a gloved hand from the window until she had disappeared round a bend in the road.

She had promised to send the photographs and they eventually arrived by post, but Adriana doesn't think they came with an address in England and if there was an accompanying letter, it was lost ages ago.

'And now I can't even remember her name,' says Adriana. 'Perhaps it will come back to me later.'

I ask her what she would have liked to study if she had gone to university and she says she always wanted to do that work in which you dig in the ground and find out how people used to live long ago.

# Destiny

Adriana says she has often wondered how her life would have unfolded if she had gone to England. It's as if her alternative destiny were still there, stretched out in front of her like a road leading through a landscape she has never visited and arriving eventually at a future as solidly real as a town that lies just out of sight on the other side of a hill.

'You might have become a *professore*,' I say and she grins at the audacity of such a thought and nods her head and says why not, everything is possible.

It's true she could have learnt English very easily and gone to university and studied archaeology or paleontology, so that within a few years she could be busy digging in the ground and finding out how people used to live long ago. It was not difficult to see her as a wise and intense academic, a different person, but still unmistakably herself.

And I can see Nella, the post office lady, as a professor of Italian history. I can imagine her peering over her spectacles with sad and affectionate eyes at a class of students all eager to know her opinion of the state of Italy in the post-war period.

And Ida and Agostina teaching in a school for girls, and sharing their enthusiasm for calligraphy and poetry and the simple fact of learning and the sense of freedom it can give you.

And when these alternative lives were over they would all have returned to the village and they would now be busy planting potatoes and pruning the olive trees and listening to the sound of the river.

For Armando it was different. He left the valley that one time when he was ten years old and he never again felt the need to go away.

# Nanda Remembers

Nanda tells me about her travels. 'I have been to so many places!' she says. In the early 1950s, before she took over the shop, she lived in France for a year or more, but then something happened and she returned to the valley. In 1986 she went to Barcelona in a bus, along with a group of other people. 'I can show you the photographs!' she says, and she disappears into the room at the back and returns with a plastic souvenir camera that provides six views of Barcelona on a little wheel. I hold the camera up to the light and press the button to look at the pictures, but they have all faded into a monotone of brown, making it hard to distinguish a cathedral from a city square.

Nanda has also been to Rome, to Bassano, to Rimini and to Venice, but when the Gulf War started she didn't want to travel ever again because the world had become too frightening.

I was in her shop this afternoon. She wasn't busy and she asked if I would like some fruit salad. Every morning she prepares fourteen portions of fruit salad in little glasses, each with its own spoon. Then as the day progresses she must decide who among her customers is to be honoured with this gift. Coffee as well perhaps, in which case you are invited into her room at the back where she has installed a new espresso machine that makes all sorts of intimate noises, ending with a little 'ping!' when the coffee is ready.

The room also contains a narrow bed covered in cuddly toys and random heaps of papers and a sink filled with things to be washed or prepared later. A round table with four chairs holds more heaps of papers and everywhere there are boxes waiting to be opened or emptied or flattened and taken to the recycling bin down the road.

So I was sitting at the crowded table in the back of the shop with coffee and fruit salad and I asked Nanda if she remembered the English lady.

She was shocked by such a silly question.

'Of course I remember her! She came to our house. Such a fine lady, so well dressed, so well mannered; her husband wore a white suit and a silk tie and a straw hat.'

'Can you remember her name?'

Nanda says she can't but she has some photographs. 'They are all in the cupboard,' she says, indicating a narrow and insecure-looking piece of furniture in a corner of the room. She sits down on a chair facing it and tugs at the handle on the bottom drawer, which resists her for a moment and then jumps out and lands on the floor with a thump. It is full to the brim with loose photos and photos in little albums and photos in those paper wallets that were used years ago.

Nanda picks up a heap of images and almost at the top of the pile she finds herself and her sister Adriana standing beside the English lady's black car, which I can now see is a Lancia. And then here she is on the same day, sitting on the wall beside the house of her childhood and smiling with her hands in her lap. She turns the photo over and on its back there is some writing in a sloping hand. *I piu cari auguri da chi sempre ti ricordi. Geltrude. Natale 1955.* 'Very best wishes from one who always remembers you' and the name with an Italian spelling and the Christmas date.

So there we are, a little mystery solved. The Englishwoman obviously kept in touch with the family for much longer than I had imagined.

A bell rings to announce that a customer has entered the shop. Nanda glances at the mirror that serves the purpose of a video surveillance camera. 'I must go. You look through the rest. Look in all the drawers. Take your time.'

I sit in her little room and open each resistant drawer in turn. There are some more pictures that must have been taken by the newly named Geltrude's husband and one of Nanda and Adriana on their way to school wearing the black-and-white Fascist uniform their father hated so much. And here is Nanda at the seaside wearing a two-piece swimming costume and smiling and smoking a cigarette, and Nanda in a summer dress smiling while dancing with a young man, and Nanda in an elegant jacket and skirt smiling on the road next to a restaurant, and Nanda in a pink overall smiling outside her shop.

The years pass and it is remarkable how little she changes with their passing. That's not quite true; when she was young she looked quite plump and insecure, but from the moment she acquired the shop she was transformed into the elegant and somehow ageless queen of a tiny kingdom. She receives her customers as if they were visiting courtiers from another land and she rarely steps over the threshold into the world beyond.

'It's very hot,' I said to her last summer.

'Yes, I saw the sun on the wall opposite,' replied Nanda, while the fan from her air-conditioning machine blew its cool breath towards her.

28 January 2007 (from my notebook):
Printed notice in our cabin on the night train to Rome:
*In the event of declenchment of audible alarm, evacuer the compartiment without precipitation and come into contact with the crew.*

30 January 2007
Pompeii in the sunshine and the energy and bustle of a town two thousand years dead. The condensation of time and no space between now and then. The streets with big paving stones worn into grooves by the passing of metal-wheeled carts and chariots, and the high stepping stones for crossing the streets, marked with the indentation of thousands of feet all landing in the same place.

20 May 2007
We were with Andreas yesterday in the mountains: sun and wind and so many flowers and he said that when you look at the enormity of the night sky, you have the sense of a distant deity with no interest in the muddles of the human struggle.

22 May 2007
Keeping Eliana company on a visit to the gynaecologist. Above the imposing desk in his consulting room he has a print in a gold frame showing two naked baby angels, the boy angel is kissing a girl angel. He has bird's wings and she has butterfly wings. They sit together on a cloud in a blue sky.

# Adriana and the Gypsy Woman

Adriana at the age of fifteen still felt as if her life were balanced on the edge of something. That was when she determined to marry Arturo.

Her mother said that people in the village spoke badly about Arturo on account of his limp, which was like a sign of bad luck. They said he would not make a good husband because he could never work as hard as other men, but Adriana wasn't interested in such arguments. She knew she loved Arturo for his gentleness and his laughter and even for his limp, which was what had drawn her to him in the first place; but she also loved him because he would make her part of his family and from now on she would belong with them.

She had failed to go with the lady to England but from that experience she had learnt to become more defiant. She told her mother that if she forbade the engagement she would simply run away to live with Arturo and

not care what people said. And with that her mother had no choice but to relent.

They became engaged, and Arturo taught her how to ride a bicycle and she sometimes went with him to visit his mother at the House of the Warm Spring. La Muta welcomed her, stared into her eyes and spoke with her lips and with the strange flat sounds that Adriana was already beginning to understand. 'You are weak and Arturo is strong,' said La Muta. 'He will look after you,' and she rubbed her two index fingers together to indicate the union.

'It was true, he did look after me

and I became strong because of him,' says Adriana, thinking of her husband and their life together.

---

They were married in the little church by the river where two angels stared out from the plastered wall, one on either side of the door. The priest performed the ceremony and Old Tunin was there in his best trousers, the sash tied tight round his waist.

Arturo had been working as a shepherd, but he said a shepherd's life was no good for a married man, so he and Adriana moved into a room in the remains of the military barracks by the river and for a while they cultivated the land that belonged to the *padrone*. But then this *padrone* lost all his money and went mad, and wandered into people's houses and sat there in a corner as if he had been invited, and his wife was no longer a grand lady and had to put on heavy shoes and an apron and grow vegetables in order to survive.

'I felt sorry for him and sorry for his wife,' says Adriana. 'The masters still owned everything, but they had all become less powerful after the war. They couldn't demand as much from us and little by little we stopped belonging to them in the way that we had before.'

The young couple moved to the village and worked in the shop, the same one that now belongs to Nanda, although in those days they had nothing much to sell except flour and chestnuts and pasta and bags of sugar. While they were there Adriana gave birth to their first child, a little girl she named Giovanna who was born in the room next to the shop and who died after a week of struggling life. 'She was so beautiful and perfect, but she was tiny and I was still almost a child myself and I had no strength.'

Shortly after the birth a gypsy woman came to the shop and said she wanted to read Adriana's hand. Adriana was terrified because of what further disasters might lie within the lines on her palm. She begged someone to run quickly for the priest, so he could make the gypsy lady go away. The priest arrived but not before the gypsy had begun pouring out her angry predictions.

---

At first Arturo had no work, so he would help his brother Giacomo who had three mules, which he took up into the mountains to fetch charcoal; a big lorry then came to collect it. One time Arturo went on the lorry and came back with a little chain necklace he had brought for Adriana; maybe it was made of silver and maybe not, but she had never been given anything before and had never owned something so beautiful.

Giacomo used to sing while he was working in the mountains and many people can remember hearing his voice from far away. He was killed one morning when he was hit by a tree that was hurtling down on a metal pulley. In the evening of that same day Adriana's son was born.

Arturo starting working in the town further down the valley and soon he was earning enough money to arrange to buy the large house known as the House of the Sea Captain. Adriana thinks it was important for her husband to become the owner of a house that had belonged to the family of his old masters. It was a question of dignity. So there they lived and Arturo worked all day and worked again when he came home in the evening. He had twelve hunting dogs, wild pigs in a shed, a tame fox that sat on an armchair and a jay that perched on his shoulder – and three more children were born.

'I was happy with Arturo, he was everything to me,' says Adriana simply. 'I was happy with my marriage and I loved La Muta more than I could ever love my own mother. But still I have often wondered how my life would have been if I had gone to England.'

She tells me about *l'uomo*, the man who sometimes comes to work with her on the land. I have met *l'uomo* a couple of times. He drives a battered Ape, one of those noisy scooter trucks, and he never speaks except to mutter a yes or a no. He keeps his head bowed and has a way of ducking his body as if he is always expecting a blow to descend on him.

'*L'uomo*'s father was not a bad man, but he was useless,' says Adriana. 'His mother drank. She gave birth to seven children. There was no food for the children, so they ate raw chestnuts and learnt to hunt for birds and eels, and they often went hungry. The mother treated them like animals and the father ignored them because he was weak.

'People in the village felt pity for the children. The wife of the *padrone* who was a marquis and lived in Rome took two of them into her care and brought them up as if they were her own. And now they live in Rome and they are fine people and no one needs to know how hungry they once were.

'Two others were taken by a rich family further up the valley and a fifth boy was sent to study in the seminary on the coast and he became a priest.

'But no one wanted the other two, so they stayed with their mother. The girl died before she was grown up and the boy became a man and worked in any way he could in order to live.

'I tell you this because destiny is very strange and I do not know who I would be now if I had chosen to go to London,' says Adriana.

# Growing Older

So many of the men and women I speak to are in their seventies and eighties. I have grown accustomed to old hands, old faces, cautious movements that anticipate the pain in the back, the ache in the legs, people who are bent forward as they walk as if they are still carrying a heavy load.

And Herman and I are growing older as well. Sometimes I realise it when we stand next to each other and look into a mirror, and I see as if for the first time how one side of his face and neck have been battered by all the cancer treatment. I see by the lines on his face and by his grey curls that he is not a young man any more, and I see by the softness of my flesh and by the lines on my face that I am not a young woman either. I look at these two familiar strangers. We are neither of us who we once were, but nor do we feel as if we are really the people we seem to have become. I suppose we have one foot in the past and one foot in the future and here we are, hovering somewhere in between.

'You are still young and I am old,' says Adriana, laughing because she feels she is ahead of me in the race to the finish.

# Talking of Life and Death

It is still very hot. There is no wind and even the crickets hold their breath and keep silent, waiting for the evening.

Adriana has been very busy with her family and with her new grandson, who is small and perfect, blinking wide-eyed at the world. But then I telephoned and she said she was on her own that afternoon and perhaps I could come and see her and maybe bring some bread from her sister in the shop if it wasn't too much trouble.

Her kitchen is cool in spite of the heat outside. The wife of the German man who sometimes frightens her when he says the word *kaput*! has given her a cake. 'Have some. It's very good,' says Adriana, 'but I don't like it, I am not used to it,' and she makes a sweeping gesture with her hand over the cake as if she hopes it might disappear.

She is full of talk. 'I have not written my diary,' she says, 'even though so much has happened: the baby, the summer. I will try to write in the winter when I have more time.

'The new baby is very small,' she adds, and he makes her think of her Giovanna who only lived for a week. 'But I must not think of her, it is not wise.' For a while she sits and is lost in thought.

'When I pray to God,' says Adriana, emerging back into the present moment, 'I ask Him not to bother with me. I ask Him not to look at me, to leave me in peace,' and she bends forward and covers the side of her face with her hand so that God cannot see her being happy because of her grandson who is so new and so vivid with life and so vulnerable.

'Fulvio, my youngest son, went to a dance,' she says, 'and two hours later I was told that he was dead. That was the second time I thought of escaping from the village. I said to Arturo that we must leave at once, he and I and our three surviving children. I said we could go on moving from one place to the next, until God couldn't see us and we had left our troubles far behind. But Arturo told me we must stay and be patient and I learnt that from him.'

192

She tells me that not long after the death of her son she and Arturo were driving somewhere in the mountains and a motorcyclist swerved against their car as he was overtaking them and the young man fell on the road. 'He was lying there,' she says, 'and I cradled this young man in my arms and he kept saying he was all right, he was all right. We took him to the nearest hospital and I sat with him on the back seat and it was as if it was my son I was holding, but this time he was not going to die.' They stayed in the hospital for long enough to make sure that everything was under control and then they left. She never asked the young man for his name or where he lived.

'I have my faith,' says Adriana, 'and that helps me. I have the photographs of my two sons and my husband beside the bed and I look at them before I go to sleep and they watch over me. They are waiting for me and when I die I know I will find them again, even if I live to be a hundred, I will find them. And I love my daughters and my grandchildren and they are here and I live for them until my time comes.

'I have had so much trouble,' says Adriana, 'that I am no longer afraid of death. I have learnt to live hour by hour. I know that I am here now, but I do not know if I will be here in the evening. Nothing frightens me now, except the rain and the wind. And mice, I am still afraid of mice.

'I was here in this house and there was so much work that I was always tired and Arturo was tired too and often in pain because of his leg, but I walked and saw two boys walking ahead of me and two girls walking behind me and I was surrounded by my own children and I was happy.'

She tells me that just a few days ago she dreamt of her eldest son Marco, and he held out his hand to her as she tried to climb a steep path. 'Take my hand,' he said, 'or you will fall,' and then she woke up shaking. She wonders if it is the dream that makes her want to talk in this way today; sometimes we need to remember things because only then can we forget.

'My mother came to live with us here when she was very ill,' says Adriana. 'But she remained angry and impatient even when she was helpless in her bed and she still had no kind words for me and no pity. But I learnt to love her and that was important because it made my heart quiet. And now I just ask for the strength to be able to continue, to walk to the end of my life.'

The conversation is over. We each drink a glass of yellow wine and I try some of the cake while Adriana watches me eating it, to see if it tastes as nice as it looks.

# God's Eye

Years ago when I was still very young, a whole stream of disasters crowded in upon me and I felt as if I was drowning from fear. At night I dreamt that people I loved had died and when I woke there would be a time of transition when I couldn't disentangle the dream from the reality. During the day I seemed to be cloaked in a kind of thick mist, which kept me distant from everything and everyone around me.

I remember feeling that I was caught in the headlights of some terrible destiny: I was being punished for sins that were maybe my own or that maybe had a history far beyond the scope of my particular life and I wanted to hide from the eye of God.

# Maps and Guns

When I arrive Armando is just shooting off in his battered black Fiat Panda to do something with the goats. 'Ida's there,' he says. 'I'll be back in a few minutes.'

Ida is pruning the ivy. 'I am trying to do it the way that Pino always did it,' she says, making uncertain snips at the tangle of greenery that covers a low wall.

It's still very hot and when Armando returns he suggests that we sit on the bench outside Ida's house.

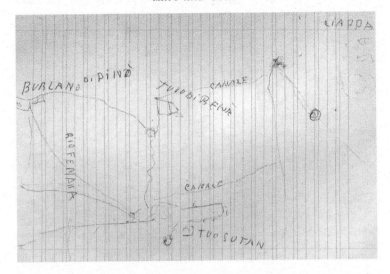

'*Mama mia!*' says Ida. 'How can I sit there where my poor Pino sat for the last years of his life? It's as if I can still see him now!'

But she sits down all the same, so here we are in a row in the shade. Neither she nor Armando are bothered by the flies which drift about in dizzy clouds and then set to with urgent couplings when they land on our arms and legs.

I tell Armando that I'd like to try to walk to Tuvo by a different way, setting out from our house, and I ask him if he could draw me a map. He takes my pen and begins by making sketchy lines on a page of my note-book. He gets excited as the map starts to take shape. 'This is Higher Tuvo,' he says, drawing a nest of little circles. 'It is also called Tuvo di Bene after my father, and this' – and he makes another nest – 'this is Lower Tuvo where my aunt came with her family.'

'The lavender. Don't forget the lavender,' says Ida. 'It grows so well on that rock below the house. I used to pick some and put it in my pocket. There were many snakes there, in the sunshine, so you had to be careful.'

'Here is Ciappa where Clelia came,' says Armando who is still busy with his map, 'and this is Burlano where the shephered kept his sheep and this is the line of the canal we built from earth, close to the river we call the

195

Fennaiia; the stepping stones must still be there and then the path begins to climb on the other side. And here is a hut and here is a threshing floor.'

'There were maybe twenty families living around Tuvo in the summer,' says Ida, 'and a man came on his donkey to collect the grapes. We could never afford a donkey but my uncle had one.'

'From when I was nine or maybe ten years old I was on my own at Tuvo every summer from May until the end of September,' says Armando. 'My brother Pino came when he could, but that was not often, and my mother visited me once a week with bread and other food, and for the rest of the time I just had the goats to keep me company. I slept with them. I didn't dare to sleep on my own in the room upstairs, the room with a window, because I was always afraid of the dark. The dog howling outside and the moon so big that I could see everything and then the owl cried and I was so frightened I thought I would die.' Armando looks at his map as if it were a photograph with the image of a little boy cowering in one corner.

We have another of these abrupt jumps in time and Armando says that when he was seventeen, in May 1944 it must have been, he was told by his father to take a twelve-year-old sheep to the house called Ciappa, which was above Tuvo. That was where the partisans were hiding and they needed something to eat, because they had nothing except for last year's chestnuts. As with all his stories, it is his own fear that he remembers so vividly.

He set off on the long path with the sheep on a string trailing behind him. He arrived at Tuvo and clambered straight up past Clelia's house until he reached Ciappa. Two partisans were on guard, watching over the whole valley. They took the sheep from him and he heard it crying out as it was slaughtered almost immediately. They set the carcass to cook over a fire and then they divided the hard meat between eighteen men. They had no salt.

As soon as Armando had eaten his small portion he was told he had been chosen to keep watch through the night. He was given a gun and instructed to make the sound of an owl if he saw soldiers passing on the road below.

The moon was full, casting pale shadows among the trees and making the entire valley brightly visible. Armando was tired and still hungry, and although he tried to keep his eyes open he quickly fell into a deep sleep and he was only woken when one of the partisans gave him a kick in the bum. He panicked, grabbed hold of the rifle and accidentally squeezed the trigger so that a shot went ringing through the night.

Everyone was immediately, awake, snatching for their weapons and convinced that yet again they had been betrayed by a spy. When they realised it was just the foolish boy who had brought them the sheep they forgave him, especially since there was no movement down below in the valley.

---

Ida has been listening carefully and now her memories are stirring and taking shape. She tells me how she and her sister had to take food to a wounded partisan. 'He was lying in a hole in the ground, not far from where we lived,' she says, her voice full of pity. 'He was lying there with terrible wounds and there was nothing to be done because it was too dangerous to bring him to the house and too dangerous to try to find a doctor. So we took a bit of food to him and left it beside him, but his head was open with a great wound and I don't think he was able to eat anything. It took him several days to die. He told us he was a male nurse, an *infirmière*, and that made it all the more sad to see him like that.'

Ida pauses. 'We were just children,' she says, 'and we weren't too upset with the idea of a man dying close by, because he was a stranger and we didn't know him. We didn't think of fear.'

She suddenly remembers that there was another wounded partisan lying on the ground somewhere near the house. He had a leg wound and people managed to carry him under the cover of darkness along the mountain paths to the place where a partisan doctor was working. The man's leg was amputated and he survived.

'Maybe the Fascists heard about what we had done, because we learnt they were coming again to look for partisans and we didn't dare to be questioned by them, so all of us, three families and eight children, went to hide in the cave known as the Tana Tsiso. It's below the path that leads to Tuvo, close to a shrine and a group of houses we called Passi, but I doubt if you could find it now. We all crawled into the hole. We had brought some dried food and we stayed there for I don't know how long. We kept quiet, until we were sure the Fascists had gone.'

---

I had promised to bring Joseph Sacco's musket with me and Armando wants to see it. Ida excuses herself, saying she hates even looking at guns and anyway she must finish pruning the ivy. I fetch the musket from the car and take it to Armando's house, placing it proudly on the table.

'Eough!' and he grabs hold of it and flips off some of the metal inlay. He gives the muzzle end a hard knock with his hand and a bit of the wood breaks off.

'It's not much good!' he says and bangs the butt end on the table, releasing a little heap of woodworm powder.

'Careful!' I say, thinking that at any moment he is going to snap it over his knee and put it in the cold stove for kindling in the winter.

With that Armando softens a bit. He takes a pair of pliers out of his pocket and gently taps the metal inlay back in place. 'I have a much better gun,' he announces by way of explanation, before going to fetch it from his cellar. He returns carrying a musket made entirely of polished metal with the fierce head of a bearded man on the barrel. 'I found it in a hole in the wall in my uncle's house,' he says, indicating the house next door, which is now owned by an Englishwoman.

Armando is talking about his uncle who had red buttons on all his jackets and was so wise he was like a priest. 'He had many books,' says Armando, knowing that I like books. 'They were bound in leather and they had pictures in them. And he had old maps and albums of photographs he had taken himself and he had paintings. There was even a painted portrait of our grandparents, which he arranged to have made.'

'What happened to all these things?' I ask nervously, imagining such fragile treasures heaped up in the same cellar from which the musket has just emerged: damp stains spreading their contours across the maps, the leather bindings of the books gnawed by rats, the photographs so faded that the long dead people are like ghosts and the wonderful portrait in its carved frame turned almost black by time.

'My uncle died when he was just fifty,' says Armando. 'We went to his house and took out all the old things that he had kept and we threw them on to a big bonfire. I don't know why, but it didn't seem right to keep anything that had belonged to him.'

# 18 April 2010

The morning had a dim look to it, the sky clear but colourless and the land without shadows as if everything was seen through a grey yellow filter, like the sky before an eclipse. We are full of thoughts of the volcanic eruption in Iceland, which is pouring into the air carrying minute particles of molten glass and I suppose that might be the cause of the diminution of the light, although it's probably just my imagination on another strangely cold day in this strangely cold year.

Armando has given me his mobile number in case we get lost while looking for Tuvo, but the way he describes it makes it seem very straightforward.

The path begins well. Another finger drawn along the flank of the mountain, a thin thread with its own metaphor of travel and distance. I imagine Armando's mother and Ida's mother and all the other strong women carrying heavy baskets on their heads, knitting socks as they walk.

In my mind I try to clear away all the thronging chestnut saplings, the brambles and the briar bushes until there is only a green carpet of meadow grass with the occasional imposing presence of a big, well-tended tree. Ida said the land was so carefully maintained that you could walk anywhere with an open umbrella. It meant that you could see so much further, looking through the widely spaced trees towards the mountain pastures that in the summer were smudged blue with lavender flowers. People calling to each other, their voices carrying across the valley and then a return to silence.

We go past an overhanging ledge of pale rock, which acts like a roof, and this must be where the carbon makers would sleep on the ground, safe from the rain. Armando said the partisans sometimes slept there too. I can't find the carbon burners' bread oven, which they used to bake a single flat loaf, although I am not quite sure what I am looking for and there are several long holes cut deep into the soft rock which I suppose might have served as an oven, or as a place to keep a knife or even a gun. Armando said there was also a high sleeping ledge with enough room for two people side by side, but I can't find that either.

And now comes a big cliff face rather like the one where the Hermit had his precarious dwelling. The rock leans out above us and appears to be put together out of loose building blocks that could all fall down if you gave them a quick kick. And here is a slab of smooth reddish stone with numerous inscriptions cut into it. I find Pino's name and surname and a date: 1938. Next to it is a drawing of a ship, about the size of two spread hands; it has sails and a little flag at its stern, but patches of lichen have spread across it making it difficult to photograph. I remember Armando told me about this ship and was very proud of it even though it was his brother who made it. There is another inscription from 1898, and someone called Battista carved his name here in 1944. All these men on the mountain wanting to be remembered, if only by an initial.

I phone Armando and tell him where we are. 'Ah! You have reached the rock we call Magraia!'

I say I have just made a photograph of Pino's ship and he sounds very pleased. 'You see, it is still there! And that means you are almost at Tuvo! Another hundred metres or so and the path will be easy to find. It's not steep. You'll see Clelia's house first and mine is only a few paces below it.'

We walk on for more than a hundred metres, but there is no sign of anything that could be called a path. I phone Armando again from a flat promontory of rock, which sticks out like a green nose. 'That is where Maria Rossa grew her lavender!' he says. 'Go a little further and you'll see the way, you can't miss it!'

Up until now a black water pipe has been accompanying us, sometimes hiding under the loose earth, then returning with its reassuring presence. The pipe continues its serpentine journey even when the path we are on has inexplicably faded away. So we follow it, for lack of anything else to follow. We reach an incongruous wooden gate, which stands all on its own in the middle of nowhere in particular and it's only then that I realise I have been here before: on the long walk Herman and I made during that first week in April 1999, when we became so lost we thought we might have to sleep curled up under a tree.

We struggle on. We have a brief glimpse of what appear to be the roofs of houses among the trees and even something that looks like the single window within an expanse of yellow wall, which Armando knew so well, but then the whole lot vanishes like a mirage and we find ourselves scrabbling up and down steep bits that lead to even steeper bits and rose bushes keep surging in and trying to surround us.

I phone Armando one last time. 'It's too long ago,' he says after a pause. 'I can't really remember how we got to Tuvo. We just went the way we always went and now it has all changed so much and even if I were with you I might not be able to find it. I am sorry.' He puts the phone down without saying goodbye.

It takes us quite a while to get back to the wooden gate, but from there we can simply retrace our steps. As we are approaching the place we started from there is a sudden snorting exhalation and a bulky wild pig crashes through the undergrowth just close to us, followed by her three striped and skittering babies.

# The Man Who Wanted to Forget

Eliana introduced me to Gian Battista whom everyone called Batti. When I held out my hand in greeting, he snatched it and put it to his lips. 'Ah, Batti!' said Eliana, laughing. He grinned and shivered with pleasure and did one of his little pirouettes.

She told me that he had grown up in our house. I asked him what it was like in those days, but a look of panic went over his face and all he would say was *miseria, miseria*, so I never asked him again. He was a member of the Sasso or Stone family and he was born in 1938, so he was just ten years older than me.

Batti ran the restaurant in the lower village for a while. That was when he was happy and living with a woman called Giovana. I am sure he must have been a wonderful host, always smiling and fluttering his eyelashes. He had a very speedy and somehow theatrical way of talking and he moved like a nervous dancer. He loved paying compliments to women, no matter what their age or appearance, so all the women loved him in return, especially since he managed to be unthreatening to their husbands or partners.

But then Giovana had died even though she was so young and Batti's heart was broken. He still fluttered and flattered, but the sadness made him more of a clown than a dancer.

By the time I met him he had stopped working altogether and lived in a single room in a house not far from here, a place that looked as if it had been abandoned years ago. The shreds of a grey lace curtain hung in the one cracked and dirty window, and the paint on the door had blistered and faded. An open storeroom on the ground level was filled with broken tools and heaps of old bottles and boxes.

Batti never got up before midday, then he would climb into his battered Fiat Panda and drive off as fast as he could in a cloud of exhaust fumes. He went to an assortment of cafés and drank a bit and talked a lot, and even though he appeared so thin and tragical, people welcomed him because they felt at ease with him.

We'd sometimes pass each other on the road and stop and talk through the open windows of our cars, or I'd see him in the upper village and he would dance towards me, his arms wide open for an embrace, his exhausted face wreathed in smiles. '*Porca Madonna*, there you are, my dear one. How are you, how is your husband? I am coming to see you tomorrow, wait for me, I'll be there. I must go now, I have an appointment.' And he'd blow kisses on his thin fingers.

'Whom are you going to meet, Batti?'

'There is a woman in Savona,' he'd say, or it could be in Milan, in Paris, in Naples or in Sicily. 'There is a woman and she is very rich and very, very beautiful. She has long golden hair and she wears fine jewels and a fur coat even in the summer and she lives in a palace and, would you believe it, she wants to marry me! Just because she loves me! Oh, you should see her eyes, the colour of the sky, and her golden hair, but I think I have already told you about her hair.'

'How are you, Batti?' I asked another time when we were both in Nanda's shop and he fluttered his lashes and did his dance and said he was very, *very* happy because finally Nanda had agreed to marry him and the wedding would be taking place next week. 'Isn't that true, my dearest love?' he asked Nanda and she turned a little pink with pleasure and embarrassment and said to me, 'Batti, but you know Batti! He is as he is, what can we do?'

---

I had heard that he was ill and was having chemotherapy and radiotherapy, but he didn't talk about it much and when we offered to drive him to the hospital he said it was all right, he could manage on his own. I met him one last time, driving up the road and he stopped his car and got out and took my hand and said there was a certain countess in Rome and he must go to see her soon because she was longing for him. But then his restless and strangely beautiful face went quiet and he told me he thought he might be dying any day now. With that he cupped my chin in his hands and kissed my forehead and returned to his car and drove off with the engine roaring.

He was taken to hospital a week later and I meant to visit him but I didn't, and I still don't know why; maybe I didn't want to believe he was never coming back. He telephoned Eliana and told her that the beautiful nurse who was caring for him had agreed to marry him and then the nurse came on the phone and giggled and said, 'Oh, Batti! You know Batti.' A big, gentle man from the village went to sit with him every day and other people went too, so he was not alone.

The funeral was held in the church in the upper village, the one that looks like a piece of iced cake. Because of restoration work that never advances from one year to the next, the inside of the church is filled with a thick forest of scaffolding, with just enough room for people to gather among the cold trunks of steel.

The priest did his best, but he said very little about Batti and a lot about sin and death and the eternal life we are all so keen to begin. My feet were cold and the metal poles with their bolted joints hemmed me in like a cage, and I felt sadder and sadder and more and more bereft because I had loved Batti in my way.

Just before the service was over, a skinny white-and-brown cat walked slowly up the aisle, its quivering tail held erect with a little kink at the end. Everyone in the congregation watched its progress and when it reached the priest in his long robes, it turned and came all the way back down the aisle and went out through the big open doors.

The coffin containing what was left of Batti was lifted with ease on to the shoulders of four pall-bearers and a murmuring crowd followed him down the cobbled track that led to the cemetery. The cat came too.

We entered the walled area of the *Campo Santo* and the priest stood in the sunlight at the far end and said some more words. As he was finishing the cat again walked slowly towards him and turned and walked back and waited. And when the coffin was lowered into the fresh grave, the cat stepped carefully round the circumference of the hole in the red earth. Then it left us and we watched it going back the way it had come.

I haven't seen it since, although the village is filled with such a mixed bag of thin cats that I don't know if I would recognise it if I did. But still, when they speak about Batti and how much they miss him, everybody remembers the cat.

# Nostalgia

Here in the valley we are surrounded by wild nature. We can walk for hours without much likelihood of seeing another human being. The nights are quiet and huge, the silence broken by the occasional cry of an owl. We have grown accustomed to the precipitous flight of the peregrine falcons whose nest is not far from here and on clear days a family of eagles move through the vast spaces of the air, the juvenile recognisable by the mottled patches on the underside of its wings. We smell the sharp scent of fox and the ripe stink of wild pig very close to the house, and there are often traces of polecats and pine martins on the terrace where we drink coffee in the morning.

But still I am aware of how much has changed. People talk about the great gatherings of toads after the rain; the bats swarming so thickly around the streetlights in the village that they almost obscure them; snails emerging in their thousands on the walls of the terraces; clouds of fireflies as bright as the sparks from the fire in the church square on Saint Anthony's day; dozens of hares racing through the little fields of corn in the mountains; eels as thick as your arm in the river.

Now only a light scattering of fireflies moves among the bushes in the months of May and June. Last summer, Adriana's eldest grandson caught an eel and everyone talked about it. Armando has a pair of red squirrels nesting in a tree near his house and I have heard that there is another pair close to where Rinuccia used to live, but I don't know of any others. We had a couple of nightingales singing at the end of our track, but recently they have gone silent and the single pottering hedgehog who emerged in the spring has vanished without trace. During the eleven years of being here I have come across just two hares in the mountains.

Only the feral cats are doing well in their lean and mean way and you are more likely to see a scrawny tabby or marmalade cat in the headlights of the car than a fox or a shuffling badger.

So that is the nature of my nostalgia and I suppose that is why I find such importance in the apparition of a hoopoe, the breeding of frogs and toads, a single salamander, or a mysterious little pile of seed-and-fruit-filled excrement.

# Finding Tuvo

When I ask Armando if we can get to Tuvo on a different path, he becomes shy with uncertainty and says he's not sure, nothing is as it was. But then one of the young men who hunts for wild pig gives us directions. We can walk there straight from our house, he says. Every time the path divides we must take the upper one and then it is simply a question of continuing.

So one morning in April, in the faded sunlight of this strangely cold spring, we again set off in search of Tuvo.

Young green catkins are dancing in the wind on thin branches. Solitary pink orchids are in flower, alongside the primroses and the delicate wood anemones. The path runs on an almost parallel line along the flank of the mountain; occasionally it is blocked by a fallen tree or lost under a little landslide or covered over by a surge of brambles, but mostly it is quite clear and easy to follow.

We go through a wooded area and emerge among wonderfully complex worked terraces, layer upon layer of them like the seats of a vast amphitheatre in a city of giants. Some of the walls have been built to a perfect straightness with quite small stones that seem to be held in a delicate but resilient balance. Other walls contain great boulders that even a group of strong men would find hard to move, let alone raise them up and place them among similar companions. There are stretches of walls built with playful curves, sharp right-angle corners and softly rounded pockets that seem to have no purpose beyond the pleasure of constructing them.

We reach a wayside shrine but it has lost the carved saint or the painting it once held. Just below the shrine we can see the heavy slate roofs of the cluster of tumbled houses, which used to be known as Passi. A fig tree, almost engulfed by thick coils of ivy, stands beside the front door of the first of the houses. Somewhere below it must lie the long cave where Ida as a young girl and all her family and the two other families crawled inside a wide space of damp and darkness to hide till the danger from the Fascists had subsided. I would like to see just the mouth of the cave, but it would mean scrambling down between the dangerous ruins of these buildings and even then I probably wouldn't find anything.

We hear the whispered barking of a roe deer, the sound distant and close at the same time, then a cuckoo and the dip-dip-dip of a woodpecker. The day is too cold for darting lizards, the quick escape of grass snakes or the lazy indolence of vipers. I keep noticing little seed-laden piles of excrement, always placed in a prominent position on a bare rock: pine martin most likely, but it could be fox.

Above the steep ravine of a stream the terraced walls have been built straight out of the perpendicularity of black rock. The stream must have once had a lot of force because it has worn the rock smooth with its passing, but now it carries nothing more than a trickle of water. Small black baby salamanders are poised motionless in shallow pools, legs splayed, big heads like the heads of fish and no yellow or red markings on their bodies as yet.

Now we arrive at a fold in the valley, which makes it more shaded. Here the terraced walls and the little fields they hold in place are all covered by a thin and uniform blanket of ivy that seems to have been thrown over them like a spell. 'Things grew wonderfully well on those terraces,' Ida told me. 'Cherries and pears, apricots and apples, and rows of grapevines that produced a special wine with its own light taste. We had three kinds of beans along with potatoes, tomatoes and cabbages; every centimetre of land was used.'

We cross a second stream and traverse a very wild and ragged forest of chestnut trees. Whole stretches of the path have been churned into a battle-ground by the snouts of wild pigs, as if they were trying to confuse the hunters who pursue them.

We emerge out of the forest and the path suddenly widens out as we approach a gathering of neat little houses, very well built with interconnecting steps and alleyways and flat garden areas where the old posts for supporting the vines are still scattered on the ground. There is a sense of gentle conviviality among the houses, making it easy to believe that the ghosts of the people who lived here still come back to sit out in the evening sun, to prune the roses and sweep the steps clean and run their hands over

the walls. The name Pipa has been carefully cut into the stone beside one of the doorways.

I suddenly realise that I have been here before, but it was years ago in a time when I knew nothing about Tuvo, so this gathering of abandoned houses was anonymous and silent.

But this is still not Armando's Tuvo that we have come to; that must be somewhere higher up. We search the steepness of the land above until we have found the faint trace of a path among the bushes of thyme and rosemary and lavender. At first I wonder if the path has been made by animals and is leading nowhere in particular, but then some way above I catch sight of the yellow stone face of a house and the little square window gazing out of the expanse of a wall, the window that made Armando cry.

The remains of a big mulberry tree is standing guard. It looks exhausted and empty of life, even though there are what seem like tight conical buds on the tips of its blackened branches. The main door to the house had gone and we don't dare to enter because the wooden floor above looks as if it might collapse with a sigh if you so much as breathed on it. We stare into the partial darkness at a long, low space with no windows.

There is an open door at the back of the house and I can see piles of old hay and a little square window with the blue of the sky coming through it.

In a separate room at the end of the building we find the shattered body of a wine barrel and next to it a metal jug stained turquoise from the sulphates used to protect the vines from mould. And that's about it.

I phone Armando to tell him we have arrived. He wants to know if the roof is secure and are there roses growing near the house and what about the mulberry tree? He speaks very fast and his voice stutters with emotion. Instead of feeling triumphant I suddenly feel as if I am an intruder, entering a place that is so much stronger in Armando's imagination than it could ever be in its derelict reality.

Going back we try a different path, which leads down to a section of the stream where there is a deep teardrop basin of water and an area where people must have come to wash their clothes on the round boulders laid out in a careful line. But the path dwindles on the other side of the stream, so we return the way we have come. The salamanders in their shallow pool are suspended in exactly the same positions as when we saw them last.

———————•———————

I took photographs of the neat houses of Lower Tuvo: the view out across the valley, the name Pipa carved into an outside wall, the little terraced gardens and steps. And I made photographs of Upper Tuvo: the first sight of the house as you approach it with the jagged outline of the mulberry tree against the yellow stone wall; the door leading to the upper room and the room from inside so that you see the square window and the sky beyond it.

I made some rough computer prints of these images as well as some

from the other Tuvo search when we got lost by the wooden gate that led nowhere. And then I phoned Ida and Armando and asked if I could show them the results of my labours.

---

We sit at Ida's table in her kitchen. Armando has brought a bottle of his yellow wine but Ida and I have decided to drink water instead. Pino with his black hair and his red lips is watching us from the picture frame on the sideboard.

I start by showing Ida a photograph of her husband's name, as it appears carved into the rock face where the charcoal burners used to stay and where the partisans sometimes came to hide. Ida cries when she reads the name and sees the date of 1938. 'I didn't even know him then,' she says, slightly perplexed.

Armando takes the picture and asks, 'Where is Pino's boat? The boat he carved on the rock next to his name?' I point to the vague bit of the prow and the mast that appear on the photograph, and explain that it is covered by patches of lichen, so it is hard to see it clearly. Armando is not impressed. He says it was a lovely boat.

I now produce the photographs of the little houses of Lower Tuvo. Ida looks at them and stops crying. She seems glad that the houses are still in one piece, but she says they are nothing like she remembers them.

Armando is not interested in Lower Tuvo, so I show him the picture I am most proud of, the one of his house as you approach it from below. He holds the photograph upside down. 'This is the cliff where the charcoal burners came,' he says emphatically, 'but I cannot see it very clearly.' Ida offers to lend him her spectacles, but he doesn't want them.

I try to tell him that this is the house of his childhood. He stares blankly at me and shakes his head. I move on to the photograph of the window taken from inside. He recognises it but says he never slept in that room. 'I was there all on my own and I was so afraid of the dark that I slept in the lower part of the house with the sheep to keep me company' – and Armando, who cries with something like longing when he holds the binoculars to his eyes and sees the pale skeleton of the house called Tuvo di Bene is confronted with himself as a lonely child, seeking comfort among the breathing tumble of sheep.

'When I ran away and came down to my family, that time when I lost the sheep, my father beat me because I was a coward,' says Armando.

------

It's almost four o'clock. Armando checks the time on his mobile phone and says he must go and collect his little granddaughter.

I stay and talk with Ida for a while. She tells me that she believes in God and prays to Him every night; then she pauses and says no, it is her husband

Pino she prays to. She says that recently Pino held her hand very tight in a dream and this pleased her because she had asked him to give her a sign that he was there, waiting for her and she had even asked him to hold her hand and then he did.

# Losing The Way

On 3 April 2010 we make one more visit to Tuvo, but now the land is thick with new growth after all the rain and everything looks different. We are so busy cutting back the brambles and snipping through tall stalks of bracken that we miss the first division of the path; we simply don't see it.

It is very warm and I use my walking stick like a blind man, testing the ground ahead of me in case there are any dozy vipers sunning themselves.

I had forgotten how far it is and how many folds in the mountain we need to cross. We pass a long terrace just beneath the path and it is thick with garden roses: blowsy pink blossoms as big as apples and the air sweet with their scent. The baby salamanders are still hanging motionless in the shallow pools of the two little streams.

Tuvo itself is also overgrown. The flat area that must have served as a tiny village square is covered with love-in-the-mist and a big frondy plant, which I think belongs to the carrot family but I don't know its name. I look inside the broken door of the house where the last time we were here we left half of one of those sandcastle cakes called *panettone* because it was too dry to eat, but there is no trace of it, not even a crumb. We have brought two bottles of sweet champagne and we place them on a stone ledge in the same house. I'm not quite sure why, but I think it was a way of leaving a trace of our presence among all the other traces. Maybe some hunters will stop here to rest, and will be glad to find the bottles, or dormice will knock them over and ants will feast on the bubbly liquid.

We eat a very odd picnic of yoghurt and marmalade and listen to the wheezing cough of a roe deer close by. The chimes of the church in the upper village are carried with a strange clarity across the bowl of the valley. Armando had told me he could hear people's voices in the evening and the voice of Agostina's mother in particular, because she shouted so loud, and as he was saying this he covered his ears with his hands as if he could hear her now.

We set off back home. Everything is familiar, the eye reminding the brain of each passing detail. Here is the hollow trunk of a tree with enough room inside to take shelter or even to sleep curled up; it looks as if someone, something, has been sleeping here quite recently, the earth smoothly compressed by the weight of a heavy body. A wild pig perhaps. We pass the rectangular stone that has been sealed within the divided trunk of a chestnut tree, and I notice a big boulder next to the path on which several small flat stones have been placed, as if left there on purpose, to communicate a message. The fact that I never saw it before makes me feel curiously disorientated.

Suddenly the path is overhung with trees and the earth is covered with white fluffy catkins, drifts of them like snow, and we are in a wide dark area of mud and stones and little pools where the pigs must congregate in quite large numbers, the mud all trampled and wallowed in. We have certainly never been here before and we don't know how we could have entered such unfamiliar territory.

We try going on, but the path stops so we retrace our steps and again we are among familiar signs: a wild rose bush we had cut back, a triangular promontory of thin grass and rock and flowering thyme, from where you can look down on our village. We turn and start again with new confidence, but we are quickly back at the pig wallow. By now the familiarity of images is beginning to overlap, the recent past and the old past superimposed on each other making it hard to disentangle the one from the other. We decide to go all the way back to Tuvo.

We sit down on the low wall beside the soft tangle and pale blue flowers of love-in-the-mist. It's as if a spell has been cast, making us lost in a place we thought we knew. There is the vague sense of being watched by those who have cast the spell. We need to find the switch, the magic world that will break the enchantment.

We set off again, but now just before entering the dark area leading to the pig wallow we notice a little oak tree with a wooden pole fixed horizontally across its top, which neither of us has ever seen before. Herman says it must be a sign of some sort, so he goes to look at it and there, falling quietly downwards across an expanse of rock to the left of the tree, lies the path we have lost. It has taken us one hour and fifty minutes to reach it, winding and rewinding our steps.

But still we keep making mistakes, twice crossing a stream at the wrong point and ending up among precarious heaps of boulders, then going up instead of alongside the stream where the terrace walls grow straight out of a steep chasm of black rock. We don't notice the mistake until we see the ruins of a huge building on our right. It seems to be of a great age, maybe because the stones are so big and smooth and the walls have not simply tumbled, but have lost a sweeping curve in a flank, revealing how thick and solid they are. There are steps leading to other buildings, but too swamped in brambles for us to try to reach them. We say how odd to have missed seeing such structures, but then we realise we have never passed this way before. Again, we retrace our steps and eventually we get home.

# PART THREE

# NOT QUITE
# FIVE NIGHTS AND
# THEN A PARTY

# A Night at Tuvo

6 June 2010

It's the first time since the Alta Via walk in 1999 that we are planning to sleep outside.

We start to make a pile of the essentials:

- matches, camping stove, a little saucepan, two green plastic cups he's had for ages, two spoons and a knife I remember buying in the Street of the Moon in Majorca in 1971.
- bivouac sack as protection from damp ground, soft rain and from wandering insects or reptiles along with two sleeping bags and a soft pink woollen wrap and a bright pink mohair blanket since the sleeping bags aren't very warm.
- two jumpers and two anoraks.
- teabags, oatflakes, an apple, a little bottle of sterilised milk because we haven't any milk powder and eight rolled-up pancakes, four with a slice of salami inside and four with lemon and sugar.
- toothbrushes, toothpaste, contact lens liquid and containers and a tiny towel.
- two litres of water, camera, notebook and pencil, spectacles, binoculars, mobile phone, a kit for removing poison in case of snake bites, insect repellent, torch – it's absurd how big and cumbersome the pile is becoming.

We pack our rucksacks and try them on. They feel much heavier than they did ten years ago.

At two in the afternoon we set off from the house. First along our track, then up a couple of zigzags on the paved road, and there is the path to Tuvo on our right, although you would never guess it was a path if you didn't know. Ida says she doesn't think she would be able to find any of the fields and houses of her childhood. 'It is as if they no longer exist, or they only exist in my imagination,' she says, looking startled by the idea that such places can be there and not there at the same time.

We each have one of those modern collapsible walking sticks and we use them a lot to keep our balance because the rucksacks make us both feel unexpectedly precarious and awkward in our movements, older than we once were.

Now it's Monday morning in Tuvo, and the church bell in our village has just chimed once, which means it's half past something, either eight or nine but most probably nine. The sound is carried up and amplified by the deep bowl of the valley, but then everything returns to silence. There are no human voices and there is not even the strange laughter of a mule or the celebrations of a chicken that has laid an egg.

I have a flat piece of slate on my lap as a writing table and my back is against a twisted mountain oak, which is growing out of the low wall I am sitting on, the roots knitted into the stones. I suppose the tree is about fifty years old, and nobody bothered to pull it up when it first sprouted from an acorn. The wall holds a flat area like a tiny village green, which is where we slept last night, and it is next to the sloping mule track that connects this group of houses and leads past them. The houses still have their roofs more or less intact, even though the wooden floors upstairs have mostly rotted away. We chose a house to shelter in if the rain came, but there was no rain, there was not even a trace of dew; everything was dry and still.

Last night I lay beside him in my sleeping bag on the ground, staring at the delicate tapestry of leaves above me as the darkness thickened. There were several owls close by, but I didn't hear the distinctive 'OoohOoooh' sound of the Eagle owl, so perhaps the three large and clown-faced owlets we saw on our way here were Long-Eared owls after all. They were wobbling and shuffling on the branch of a high tree, fluffed up to make themselves look bigger. As we approached they precipitated themselves into the air, one after the other, with a startled clatter and some odd squeaking. I wonder if we were the first humans they had ever encountered.

The other meeting was with a small toad sitting on a stone in the second little stream crossed by the path. It was so still and so perfectly camouflaged that I almost stepped on it. As my foot wavered dangerously close it shifted a few centimetres to one side and went on staring into a faraway toad-distance.

When we arrived at Tuvo, we left our half-unpacked rucksacks on the wall where I am now sitting and walked down to the round pool to fill our water bag. I thought there was a snake wriggling in the pool, but it was only a branch brought to life by the movement of the stream. Without too much anticipation I undressed and half fell, half jumped in, laughing from such an icy embrace. I wish I felt more at ease with my ageing nakedness, but it always startles me to see how much my body has softened and changed during the last years.

We got back and became quite domestic in our new home. Herman made tea, while I cleared some earth and dead leaves from the stone seat by one

of the houses and sat there and thought of others sitting there, telling each other stories in the evening. I peered through a gaping doorway into the house and counted sixteen pipistrelle bats hanging from the bits of reed that still covered the ceiling. They were like fruit, each one attached by what appeared to be a single stalk, twizzling this way and that, as if a breeze was blowing at them, although the air was quite still and they were making their own breeze with the twizzling. One of them lifted its head up towards me, a tiny enquiring face, the eyes shining with pinpricks of light.

We made our way to a little promontory looking out over the valley and constructed a stone bench from a long piece of slate balanced on two boulders. There we sat and watched the lines of the mountains drifting into shades of powdery grey. A cloud was floating like a puff of breath above the mountain that has the profile of an old man with his mouth open.

We had cold pancakes and more tea for supper, then crawled into our sleeping bags and lay there in the quiet. There was no moon visible but a brightness stayed in the sky until midnight, or at least I kept drifting in and out of sleep and seeing the brightness around me until I had heard the twelve chimes of the church bell. Some sort of animal rustled through the bushes and made a shrieking sound that I couldn't identify, but there were no wandering herds of wild pig snorting with amazement when they caught our scent. In the morning the bats had returned to their hanging places, but now there were only nine of them.

We had porridge for breakfast before scrambling up to Armando's house. At one point we lost our way and were very precarious, balancing on thin ledges above steep drops, but then there was the house, the same only different because everything had put out leaves and new shoots. Armando had asked about the mulberry tree and I had not been sure if it was even alive, but now I saw that it was covered with small unfolding leaves and clusters of tight green fruit. The roses were in bloom. He had asked about them as well.

We wanted to reach Clelia's house and the one above that where Armando brought the old sheep for the partisans to eat, but although we climbed as high as we could up the almost vertical rocks, there were no broken remains of terraces to show where people had been and not the slightest sign of a ruined building.

We set off back and this time we did not get lost. The same toad was sitting on the same rock as if he had never left it and again he didn't move when he saw us, just gulped and stared and stood his ground. No baby owls. We heard the heavy crashing of wild pigs, but didn't see them.

I went to visit Armando and Ida a few days later. He was glad about the mulberry tree and he laughed about the weight of a heavy rucksack. Ida wanted to know if I had been afraid during the night, while Armando wanted to know if I had changed. I said I wasn't sure if I had changed or not and the vagueness of my answer seemed to satisfy him.

He then asked if I believed in destiny. He said that he believes our destiny decides when we are meant to die and because of that he is not afraid of his own death. I have the feeling he quite looks forward to it, just as long as he is at home and not in a hospital among strangers.

# A Night at Carmo

12 June 2010

Another morning after another night and now we are sitting side by side on the steps of Old Tunin's house, right up on the high crest of the mountain. The rounded bulk of the old volcano where gentians and cyclamen flowers grow in such profusion is facing us from across the divide of the valley and we can also look down towards the distant sea and up almost as far as the cul-de-sac end of this little kingdom.

We came by car, following the narrow winding road as far as the point with a steep wall and a perfect hairpin bend they call *il girone*; then we parked and took out our rucksacks and sticks. It had been windy all day, but here at a height of some twelve hundred metres the wind had become really fierce and erratic in its movements as it swung and surged this way and that.

We followed the little sheep path that threads along the contour of the mountainside, very conscious of the awkward burden of the rucksacks, and when we emerged on to the first ridge there was such a sudden blast of wind that we were both almost knocked over. We sat down side by side like toddlers, shocked by the knowledge that we could have fallen to our deaths or at least to the breaking of several bones, made helpless by the weight of our tortoise packs. Old Tunin's grandson Sergio had told us how his little brother fell here once. He was sitting on the back of the donkey behind

two wooden water barrels and plopped off, and stopped himself from rolling by holding on to some tufts of grass just before a perpendicular drop. Old Tunin could do nothing and he went on crying in despair even after the boy was again there beside him.

So the wind and the thin path and me walking ahead, I suppose because I felt I was less precarious than him and I moved loose stones to one side so he wouldn't trip on them and every so often I stopped to watch him approach. He was being very careful and slow because of his tendency to trip, which he has always done very easily, but here there was no room to tumble and pick yourself up and laugh.

The wind was like a big enthusiastic dog, knocking against our legs and leaping up with its paws on our shoulders before bounding off. But the light was beautiful as it shifted in and out of the racing clouds, and as we approached our destination the flattened grass was glistening and rippling in the sunshine like fast-running water.

We were welcomed by this broken fragment of a house. Just the one small room with a solid door and a couple of big slates on the earth floor and enough space inside for two people to lie side by side. There's the fireplace in one corner with dried branches and the charred remains of a wooden beam ready to be used.

I swept away the dry mud and cow dung on the floor with a bit of a branch to make a flatter surface and we removed a few stones and the shards of the broken clay pot that I had noticed before. We took a couple of the beams outside to make more space. We decided to move one of the slates on the floor and put it back later, but when we lifted it up there was a carefully shaped deep hole beneath it – perhaps not enough space for a man to hide in, but enough to hold provisions of dried food and guns too. I remembered that Tunin had told me there were always supplies hidden here but he hadn't said where. We lowered the slate back into its old position and cut handfuls of grass to soften the floor and turn it into a sort of bed. I picked some lavender and wild thyme and now the air was filled with their sweet scent.

We sat side by side on the stone steps, and again we ate pancakes and this time we had remembered to bring bouillon cubes, so we had hot soup to drink. We sat some more, watching without really looking at anything in particular. Two cuckoos were answering each other and some warblers were warbling. A trail of tiny ants was making its determined way to where a splash of soup had fallen on the earth. We went on sitting as the evening gathered in and the outline of the mountains went dim and the wind battered around us. It was as if we had turned into Old Tunin and La Muta with no words between us and no thoughts either because the wind had carried them all away.

The wind had also carried away any mosquitoes and that night I moved quietly in and out of sleep, shifting my body on the hard floor with its tilting uneven surfaces and waking briefly with my face close to the rough stone wall so for a moment I didn't know where I was, or even quite who I was, but I was asleep again before I could try to unravel that problem.

And then the early light coming in through the open door and the soft green of the land and the grey curls of his head beside mine and we wriggled out of our sleeping bags and stepped outside into the morning.

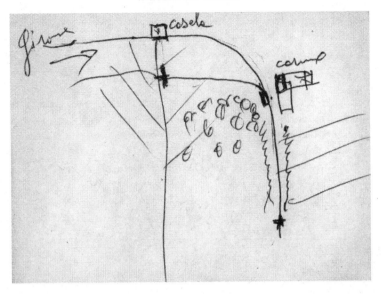

Sergio had told us how to find the path that led to a little stream where we would find a bit of water. He said it would take us a quarter of an hour to walk there, but it took us an hour and a half of cutting and hacking our way along the faint thread of the path, which had been almost annihilated by broom and thick grass, by hazelnut bushes and alder and mountain willow and the occasional pine tree. We kept catching the stink of fox and we saw the occasional foraging marks of pig and there was one pine tree with a triangle of space between its divided trunk, the bark worn smooth and greasy by the pigs who had used it to scratch their bellies and their bristly flanks. By now our hands were tired and blistered from cutting with secateurs and when we finally reached the stream bed it was nothing but a dry stain of little stones with not even a trace of dampness.

We returned to the hut and packed our things, careful not to drink all of the little water that we had left. The journey back to the car took less than two hours, but the day had become very heavy and still, with the white mist of clouds creeping around us. I felt suddenly exhausted but I kept striding ahead, as if to escape from my own tiredness. And then I'd sit down to watch my husband's much more steady approach. I collected the flowering heads of some plants whose names I did not know.

---

I told Adriana about our night out and she thanked me as if I had given her some wonderful present. 'I wish I could have come with you,' she said, 'but now you know what it is, how we felt to be there.' A few days later I phoned Tunin, just back from hospital and the fourth – or is it the fifth – operation on the metal plate in his hip, which keeps slipping out of place. 'I wish I could have come with you,' he kept saying, his voice stuttering with emotion.

# Abandoning an Idea

20 June 2010

For the third of these five nights I wanted to sleep in a village high in the mountains. It has a main street flanked on both sides by big three-storey houses and there is a scattering of other houses built around a broad flat meadow the size of a football pitch. It also has walled terraces, great tiers of them in all directions much wider than any you might expect in this steep landscape – and the people who lived here were not *mezzadri*, but owned whole swathes of land and were rich in wheat and wine and vegetables, in cattle, sheep and goats.

After the First World War, when a military base and a road were built along the crest of the mountains defining the border between Italy and France, soldiers as well as the supplies for the soldiers followed the mule track that passed close by the village, so there was always constant talk and activity and the movement of strangers.

The village had a nearby spring for water and further down the steep slope where the stream joined the main river there was a flour mill next to a humpbacked Roman bridge, and close to the ruin of an ancient building that was once a friary, the inside walls painted blue and covered with wonderful images of saints.

Three other villages were quite close by, one at roughly the same altitude but a bit further up the valley and two by the river. Families were intertwined within these communities: an uncle living here, a sister married there, grandparents in the downstairs rooms, their children and grandchildren above them. Everyone walked the paths to the same school and attended the same church and they all buried their dead in the same holy ground.

People began to leave during the aftermath of the Second World War; then the new road came, creeping inexorably along the steep flank of the valley, and that made leaving much easier. They could watch the road from a distance and see a diminutive car or lorry trundling over its asphalted surface, but to reach it they had to go down to the river and cross one of the three narrow bridges and make the laborious climb on the other side. There was nothing to be done, the modern world was passing them by. Many more began to leave, carrying a few possessions on their backs and on the backs of donkeys. Others held on until they couldn't manage any longer, or they remained and died in their houses and their houses died with them. The front doors were locked and the key was taken away as a symbol of ownership, or the doors were left open, the table set for the midday meal, flour in the flour chest, wine in the cellar. Time stopped and was held suspended, waiting to be set into motion again with the moment of return.

---

Armando told me how he visited this village with his father in December 1948. He met an old couple whose children and grandchildren had left for France. The old couple lived in a house on the main street. They had a cow and a donkey and a vegetable patch, and they grew their own wheat and transported it to the nearest mill, which was much further away than the one by the bridge that had closed down.

Armando said they had two big juniper bushes growing on either side of their front door and because it was then almost Christmas they had decorated these bushes with tiny dried apples and old bells that had once hung round the necks of goats, and a tin coffee pot and two Roman-style oil lamps, which were carefully positioned so they could be lit for a few hours at night.

The old man asked Armando if he could bring him two little nails the next time he happened to pass by and a few weeks later Armando came with a paper bag filled with the pasta called *chiodi* or little nails, which are cooked in soup; the old man was very disappointed with the gift because he had really wanted just the two nails, to mend his shoes. He asked Armando if he could climb on to the roof of the house to push a loose slate back into place. He said they were becoming lonely now that the village was almost empty and it was hard to keep going. When Armando went to the house again, he found the coffee pot on the table with cold coffee still inside it and there was a salami hanging from a hook on the ceiling and everything else was in its place as he had remembered it, but the old people had vanished.

A man known by the name of Mad Luis was also living somewhere close by at that time, along with his wife and their six children, but Armando didn't meet them. The eldest and the youngest of the children were very clever, and one became the manager of a bank and the other became a professor of medicine, but the four middle children were blind. They were not born blind; the tragedy of sightlessness overtook them gradually and inexorably. Then in 1956 the wife, who was a big round-bodied woman, stumbled and fell all the way down the steep slope towards the stream and the fall killed her. Mad Luis and the six children commemorated her death with a stone monument. They only stayed on for a while before they too moved away.

We first went in search of the village on a clear, bright day in February 2009. From the road we could just make out what seemed like the tips of broken buildings clinging to the side of the mountain and encroached on by trees. We began by following a mule track that passed a bathtub filled with sodden loaves of white bread floating in the water. A dead mouse was poised spreadeagled on the water's surface like a sky diver surrounded by clouds. We crossed the bridge and saw the ruins of a mill, which we then didn't know was a mill. We reached three empty houses, where the sheep and goats had gone in through the open doors and had moved from room to room, breaking wine bottles and barrels in the dark *cantina* and entering kitchens and bedrooms, knocking over chairs and skidding on saucepan lids, trampling on beds and getting all tangled up with old clothes and blankets.

We clambered down to a big building below this one that looked as if it had been a very fine house and the one room we could look into contained cupboards and chairs painted in white, blue and gold and a double bed with a curved wooden headboard. The covers from the bed had been thrown over a metal bar that crossed the room below the ceiling and the pattern on one of the covers showed jolly blue sailing boats bobbing on a blue sea.

We returned to the track and after a few more bends we took a little path, which seemed to be heading towards the village we were looking for. The path quickly disappeared into a maze of goat tracks and we didn't know how to continue until we saw a rounded white shape directly above us and as it were looking down on us, so we steered towards it, pulling ourselves up from one broken terrace to the next with the help of the broom bushes, which are soft to hold and have very strong roots.

We reached the stone memorial to the mother of the four blind children. It stands all on its own on a small area of flat ground, with no sign of human habitation anywhere close by; just the mountains above and the steepness of the slope below and the isolation of it all. A little gated alcove built into one side of the memorial contains a broken vase for flowers and a faded photograph of a large woman with a very serious expression. Two of the other sides are covered with a thin layer of cement on which

horizontal lines have been drawn as if these were pages in a textbook and the story of the tragedy is carefully written on the lines.

By clambering up some more broken terraces we entered the wide meadow, but we still could not see any sign of human habitation. Clumps of briar roses were every-where, but there was enough room

between each plant to thread past them and we eventually saw the remains of the street of tall houses. Here the roses were mixed with brambles and Russian vine, creating a thick fortress of spikes and prickles and rope-like tendrils, which made it impossible to approach.

We went back more or less the way we had come, but the solemn beauty of the place and the sombre authority of the memorial and the story it told stayed in my mind and made me want to spend one of our five nights there.

---

We returned on 20 June 2010. We brought three extra bottles of water which we planned to leave in a sheltered place, so we would have less to carry when we arrived the next day with sleeping bags and a tent and food.

The weather was very hot and humid, and the last stage of the climb to the village was exhausting. The memorial to the mother of the blind children no longer appeared like the dignified witness to a lost time; it just seemed unutterably sad and desolate, and I could hardly bear to look at it. Thanks to the recent rain, the briar roses on the meadow had sent out sharp and questing shoots in all directions and it was hard to avoid being scratched by them.

We approached the line of houses and managed to carve a way through the maledictions of brambles and briars until we were in the main street but balanced on a thick and twisted net of Russian vine, which held us a couple of metres above the ground. One of the vines tripped me up and I fell and landed heavily against a stone. I felt like crying both from the pain and from the savage desolation all around me.

We went round to the front of the houses and that way we were eventually able to get close to one of them. We could enter by a door that led into a big cow stall, the hay still heaped on the floor, along with old shoes, a tin chamber pot and a pitchfork. We climbed cautiously up the outside stone steps and peered through a window at heavy wooden chests and cupboards, a long table, and a shelf on which stood an oil lamp and a box that had once contained sugar.

We searched in all directions for some trace of the mule track along which soldiers and villagers had once travelled in noisy groups, but there was nothing to indicate what once had been and we got completely lost and ended up sliding down stretches of the slope on our bottoms.

We had planned to set out with a tent and sleeping bags on the very next day, but then the rain came, a cold heavy rain that seemed to have nothing to do with the month of June. It continued to rain sporadically for several more days and the apricots and cherries on the trees we planted in 2003 were splitting open before they were properly ripe, and the few fireflies that had survived the long cold of winter stopped blinking their feeble SOS messages from the bushes. We gave up the idea of spending the night in that village and felt very relieved once the decision had been made.

# Supper with Giovanin

25 June 2010

We are sitting on a terrace in the area known as Piani di Colombo, which is where Giovanin the shepherd is mostly based during the summer months. A shield beetle, its back the shape of its name, glimmering in green and gold, is walking across my shoe and a little spring-tailed something or other has just drowned in my cup of tea. Two speckled butterflies, mating tail to tail and so facing in opposite directions, have landed on the sleeve of my shirt and they stand there, uncertain about what to do next. Grasshoppers, bees, ants, beetles and spiders, everything around us is busy with activity, even the grasses and flowers are nodding and ducking, twitching and waving.

We arrived at six this evening. We parked the car close to the inside edge of the narrow road that runs just below a scattered cluster of tiny buildings used by shepherds and by their flocks, and this settlement is so perfectly hidden within a fold of the mountain that you would never know it was there until you had reached it. We set off up a track, carrying our rucksacks and not minding the weight because we hadn't far to go. Lines of tumbled walls were all around us and it was hard to distinguish between the walls of terraces, the enclosures for animals and the delicate remains of little dwellings.

Now we were entering Giovanin's territory and here was his parked jeep with the windows tightly shut and the long low structure where he sleeps in a room no bigger than a double bed, the rough stone walls as protection from the wind and a sheet of plastic suspended above the ancient mattress to keep out the worst of the rain because the old slate roof no longer serves much of that function. His flock of sheep and a few goats inhabit the space next door, so he can hear them shifting and stirring, coughing and bleating through the night.

When he is here, Giovanin does most of his cooking over an open fire in a tiny stone shelter, but he does also have an incongruous prefabricated metal garage, or 'box' as they call it, which must have originally been transported here with a tractor and trailer. Some years ago Eliana brought me here and took the key from its hiding place and opened the door to the box and we looked inside. There was a makeshift kitchen with a cold-water tap, a Calor gas cooker, a single light bulb that runs from a small solar panel, a table, wobbly benches, a few plates, cups and glasses and a supply of dried food in the cupboard. There was a door leading to a bedroom at the back. Eliana said Giovanin never slept here and didn't use the kitchen very much, but he was happy for people to make a meal here if they wanted and they could also occupy the bed for a night, if they knew him well enough to know where he hid the key.

There is no sign of him now, but we can hear the distant music of the bells on his animals. We go on up the track. We pass a little ruined house that

belongs to Giovanin's brother, who is one of the last people in the area who still knows how to build dry-stone walls, although he hasn't exercised his skill here because his house is in the process of disappearing. The roof has collapsed and a flowering elder tree is growing among rubble in the small internal space. The wall closest to the path is leaning out from the body of the building and looks as if it is about to fall in one solid mass at any moment. There is a date carved into the stone lintel above the doorway, which has lost all trace of a door: 26 August 1883.

We have brought a tent with us because the weather is still so shifty. It's the same tent Herman has had for ages and ten years have passed since we last used it when we were doing our first explorations of the valley. He keeps it and all the other camping equipment in an aluminium suitcase which once belonged to an SS officer in Germany; it had incongruously been given to his second wife's Jewish parents at the end of the war, when they were leaving the devastation of Europe on their way to a new life in America. The tent smells a bit musty, but no mice or rats have chewed holes into it, so that's good.

We choose a terrace that looks out across the bowl of the valley. From here we can see the two churches on the square in the upper part of our village, the cypress trees in the churchyard, the ridge on which Tuvo lies, the dip on the crest of the mountain that hides Old Tunin's house; we can even see the roof of Giovanin's winter home.

The swifts are screaming through the air. Herman begins to set up the tent and realises that most of the metal pegs have disappeared, so it won't

be all that stable. I lay out some flat stones on which we can place our little stove and the water bottles. I gather the heads of some flowers I want to identify later. Within a few minutes I have a brilliant orange petal from the Carnic Lily, alongside yellow Arnica, white Mountain Dog Daisy, purple Scabious, blue Bellflower, red Rampion, dark blue Sheepsbit, purple Viper's Bugloss and the almost luminous pink of Rock Storksbill. I put these little treasures in a plastic bag with a bit of water so that they don't dry out and become unrecognisable.

The scattered houses that lie so haphazardly around us are backed by a cliff wall of layered stone with a lot of crystals embedded in its surface. The presence of the wall seems to unite the village and make it feel comfortable and protected even in its present state of abandonment. I know that one of the sheep pens here dates from the Neolithic period, but I don't know which one it is and it's hard to distinguish the old from the very old.

I get out the binoculars and by scouring the smooth green surface of the mountain pastures behind us I eventually identify the skittering line of Giovanin's flock, high above, but moving slowly in our direction. A quick bark leads me to the movement of his two black dogs and then I can see him, standing at a distance and leaning on his stick, a cotton cloth tied round his head, a little cloth sack hanging from one shoulder.

An hour or so later and his dogs run towards us, barking a warning, then the two black ones come closer, their tails wagging, their heads bowed in friendly submission while the shaggy brown one keeps its distance. We walk down to meet Giovanin, carrying a bottle of wine and a couple of little salamis, and here he is, a thin man with a thin face and intensely blue eyes, the cloth that all shepherds seem to wear tied round his head like a turban. 'Ah, company!' he says, raising his hand in greeting. 'I wasn't expecting company.' I thought he might be shy of visitors, but in his quiet way he seems delighted.

'The sheep won't be coming down to be milked for another hour,' he says. 'There is time for a meal. And wine.'

He invites us into the metal box room. He doesn't like the look of our bottle with its cork and label and fetches one of his own instead, along with a packet of sweet biscuits. He pours the wine. 'Eat! Drink!' he says. 'To your health!' and we sit at the wobbly table on wobbly chairs and clink our glasses.

'Pasta! I usually only have soup, but we shall eat pasta! You two must prepare the sauce while I light the fire and set the water to boil.'

He disappears to the back bedroom and emerges carrying a little tin of tomatoes and a very little tin of something with a picture of a cow on it and an onion and a plastic ice-cream box containing a withered heap of some twenty *gambi secci*, the tiny 'dried legs' mushrooms that can be found hiding in the high pastures if you know where to look.

He shows me how to break off the brittle woody stalks and says the caps must be soaked for a while, so I pour water into a flowered teacup without a handle. Herman opens the tins and tips their contents into a frying pan while Giovanin stands by, cutting bits of onion into the pan with his penknife.

He goes to make a fire in the lean-to building, snapping the sticks over his knee with a little grunt to coincide with the moment when the wood cracks. Within seconds the flames are eager to begin their work, curling round an old black cauldron that hangs from a chain.

He disappears and returns, holding a big round cheese in both hands, from which he cuts thick slices with his penknife. It is soft and sweet and delicious. He says he eats a kilo of cheese every four days. 'They say cheese makes you fat!' he says, patting his thin torso.

He breaks the pasta in half and puts it to boil in the cauldron. He moves very quickly. 'Ah, company, I do not often have company. We shall have a feast!' he keeps saying, but he doesn't look at us when he speaks, it is just a commentary on the situation.

Maybe out of politeness he asks Herman to test if the spaghetti is cooked enough, then he drains it and tips it into a plastic bowl and mixes in the sauce. He serves us first, then himself and we begin. You can taste the mild earthy flavour of the *gambi secci* and they are nice to chew. Giovanin doesn't address us by our names and he asks no questions about how we live and nothing about what we are doing here this evening.

He begins to talk and it's as if he is thinking aloud. He says there used to be two hundred people in the Plain of the Dove at this time of the year, so many of them, so much noise and activity, he shakes his head from side to side and laughs with the recollection of laughter. There were eight shepherds and their families, then all the others who came for the lavender, for the wheat, for taking a few animals out to graze. 'Eh!' he says, 'and now I am the only one left.' With that he closes his blue eyes for a moment, as if to shut out the reality of this fact.

'There were ninety-three shepherds in the valley and between us we had thirty thousand animals,' he says and he begins to move in his mind through the names of all the villages, counting the shepherds in each one, then counting the number of their sheep and goats as if they are lining up in front of him. Five from his winter village and nine from our village, including Adriana's husband Arturo. When he mentions Arturo by name he suddenly remembers how fast he could eat, he could eat even the hottest soup in a few moments. Giovanin makes a movement with his hand to indicate the speed, then he shakes his head because those times are over and Arturo is dead. He returns to count the shepherds: four from the village opposite the bridge, twelve in the high village at the end of the valley, on and on until they have all been accounted for.

'*Povero noi!* (Heaven help us!)' he says and there is an incantatory quality in his voice, as if he is part of a congregation answering a priest. Heaven help us from the changes that have come, the silence, the loneliness, the empty houses, the trees that have grown on terraces that should be carrying wheat and vines, the tree that grows in the room of my brother's house, the desolation that has come to the mountains.

'*Bellin!* (Fuck it!),' he says because of the bureaucracy that hems him in on all sides, making it impossible for him to sell his cheeses fairly or to have his animals slaughtered, threatening him with a fine for any slight infringement of the technicalities of the law. He can't even sell the wool and is lucky if someone takes it from him and uses it to put round their olive trees. *Bellin! Bellin! Bellin!* Like the chiming of little bells.

I ask him when he first decided to become a shepherd. 'In my mother's belly,' he replies at once and without smiling. His mother was a shepherd from the village right at the end of the valley, the one built on the edge of the high cliff, and all her family before her for generation upon generation. 'There have always been shepherds in this valley,' he says with quiet authority.

And with that thought of time past, Giovanin speaks of history. He was born in 1935, so he doesn't remember much of the war, but he remembers how people cried when the young boys were killed and there were the others who were locked into a house and the house was set alight. 'Mussolini was close by, on the Pass of the Half Moon,' he says, nodding his head in the direction of the pass an hour's walk away. 'And Napoleon fought one of his battles at the same pass. When I was young I found things, bits of uniform and the bones within the uniforms, all belonging to Napoleon's soldiers.' He shakes his head with the memory of what he found and pauses for a moment, then he says there is a special stone on the ridge above this place. He stands up and raises his hand above the height of his shoulder to show how tall the stone is. He was told it was put there by shepherds thousands of years ago. There is also the altar stone in that dip in the land just below the high stone. That is where sacrifices were made, a bowl cut into a big table of rock to hold the blood and a channel cut into the rock, for the blood to flow down. 'I don't know if they were sacrificing people or just animals,' he says.

By now the sheep and goats have returned. All ninety of them stand outside the open door, taking it in turn to peer in, curious to see what's going on and why Giovanin is being so slow with his meal.

'I haven't had such a feast for a long time,' he says, speaking as much to his animals as to us.

'I am making ricotta tonight, after the milking,' he says. 'I probably won't be finished until one in the morning. I must hurry.'

It's just after nine o'clock when he goes outside. One of the black dogs skitters joyfully at his heels, nipping at his shoes as if his master were a big sheep. 'They don't work!' he says of these two sleek, gentle and endlessly willing and obedient animals who dance attendance on him like houris in paradise.

As soon as they see him, the sheep begin to file into a stone compound, talking to each other in soft voices. A round moon is rising and almost transparent clouds are moving through the dark enormity of the sky.

Giovanin carries his bucket to a narrow opening at one end of the compound and there he sits down on a little piece of wood, which is placed like a cushion on a stone ledge.

I have been told that his sheep and goats all have their own names and will answer and come to him if he calls them, and that they always line up in the same sequence, so he knows which one is next. They have turned quiet, concentrated, busy with the task of the evening and it's as if they are consciously taking part in the ritual of milking. Their heads shift and move like the waves on a choppy sea. A huge black billy goat with shaggy glistening fur and a long flowing beard moves among his ladies, exchanging polite greetings with them, or so it would seem. A couple of rams with twirling horns are also busy with their ladies. There is a sense of contained excitement in the air, like a queue waiting to go into a cinema.

One by one Giovanin allows his animals to enter the narrow gap where he is sitting; the young ones and the males pass through unbothered, the females pause while he grabs hold of a right hind leg with his right hand and begins to milk with his left hand. The ones who are next in line press their shoulders against his shoulder, their chins and noses rub against his cheek and into the cloth that covers his head. He doesn't speak to them, but they seem to be listening to him.

The black billy decides to go through the gap and he gently pushes his big body past the sheep who is being milked and settles himself close to Giovanin on the other side, sitting upright, his long neck and silky beard silhouetted by the light of the moon. I watch as one of his white wives comes up to him. She lifts a front foot and places it on his back, holding it there for a moment. She rubs the side of her head down his flank and along his neck in a repetitive gentle sweeping gesture and he sits perfectly still receiving the homage.

The moon shifts in and out of a flurry of cloud. A black nanny goat, with little wattles under her chin, keeps coming so close that we almost touch foreheads. She lifts her face towards mine, her nose twitching as she breathes in the smell of me. I wouldn't be very surprised if she spoke in a soft goatish voice, asking what sort of a creature I might be and what on earth I am doing here. Giovanin is silent within the silence, so the only sound is the soft rush of milk into the pan, each animal producing a different note.

A big mouse – or maybe it is a little rat – darts erratically along the wall and stops close to Giovanin. The dogs watch the rat until it bustles away.

By now a wind is blowing and the air is turning really cold. At ten twenty we decide to leave, so we call out a farewell to Giovanin. He wishes us a good night's rest and we walk slowly to the tent and take off our heavy boots and brush our teeth and clamber into our sleeping bags. It starts to rain and the wind is pulling and punching so fiercely at the tent that I think it might collapse. Right on the edge of sleep I imagine the two of us walking bedraggled through the dark to Giovanin who is boiling the milk for the ricotta in a big copper pan to ask if he will give us shelter and he nods his head towards the bedroom behind him. Then, when I have entered sleep, the noise of the wind gives me a dream in which I am driving through an underground courtyard in New York and there are cars all around me, hooting and shuddering and the advertising hoardings on the walls are covered with stories about Philip Roth who has done something, maybe he has just died . . . I wake briefly with the first light of dawn because the dogs are barking. Herman is awake as well and we talk a bit and he looks at his watch. It's five minutes past five. Giovanin's day must have just started.

When the sun is up we have our breakfast, sitting on grey stones, staring and hardly speaking. We walk down to Giovanin's just in time to see his animals collected in a tight and eager flock. He has the cloth sack on his shoulder and the stick in his hand and is about to lead them away. 'I am going,' he says and sets off in long strides, the animals following at a respectful distance.

# The Funeral Path

## 30 June 2010

Today we go by car to the village perched on a cliff at the head of the valley. A few people are milling about in the main street, but I don't see any sign of Eduardo, the old man who is here all through the year. Like everyone from this place he comes from a long line of shepherds, but there was too much trouble after the war, so for a while he lived with Old Tunin and La Muta. Then he went across the border into France. He got work as a builder, mixing cement with his bare hands that are now swollen and buckled and shaped like wounded claws, although he says they don't hurt much. He returned to his village as soon as he was able to retire.

Earlier in the year, Adriana had wanted to see him again and so we went together.

'Who are you?' he said, watching her approach.

'I am the wife of Arturo who was the son of Tunin.'

'You are, I recognise you! And Arturo, how is he?'

'He is dead, he died six years ago.'

'I am sorry to hear it. He was a good man, pure gold.'

'I was married to him for fifty years and then he died in an accident,' said Adriana, her eyes fluttering and seeming to turn inwards as she remembered all that had happened.

She presented Eduardo with a packet of biscuits, which she had brought for the occasion. He offered us some wine, pouring it into battered white plastic cups. We drank each other's health and then we left and he watched us go, holding up a damaged hand in a gesture of farewell.

---

But now we don't see Eduardo, so we drive on past the village until we reach the Sanctuary of San Antonio, the saint of the desert. People are fond of him because they say a shepherd's life is close to the life of a hermit in the desert.

The sanctuary looks very quiet and self-possessed and its blue painted door is firmly locked. I have been told it contains a deep stone tomb; the bodies of those who died during the winter were lowered inside this cold sepulchre and left there until the snows melted in the spring. Then the bodies were lifted out, placed in coffins and carried over the crest of the mountain and down a long winding path on the other side, all the way to the cemetery in what is now the French village of La Brigue.

It's a five-hour walk to get there and almost a six-hour walk to get back again, but the two villages were always bound together as one unit until the border between France and Italy was finally redrawn in 1947. The people shared the same family names and spoke the same dialect and herded the same hump-nosed sheep on the summer pastures. They also buried their dead side by side in the one burial ground. The man who told me about the sanctuary said that before it was built, the bodies of those who died during a cold winter were packed in snow until it was possible to move them, or they were wrapped in a cloth and lowered into deep caves in the limestone cliff, the same caves that housed the bones of the Neolithic shepherds who had also wandered with their herds through this vast landscape.

---

We leave the sanctuary and start up the mule track that Herman came down all those years ago, when the snow on the crest forced him into the valley. The air smells of strawberries. I pick a few tiny red fruits and the fleeting intensity of their sweet-sharpness is like the taste of nostalgia, if nostalgia can be said to have a taste. We see several wild apple trees, although maybe they are not wild, but were planted to provide food for people passing by.

There are also plum, cherry and walnut trees, all straggling and neglected.

I keep thinking of a column of people carrying a coffin on long poles between their shoulders. The path is gentle enough to allow them to walk with slow dignity and when there is the occasional steep ascent, the cobbles keep them from slipping. Do they sing as they walk, or talk to each other in soft voices, or is there that stunned silence of loss all around them, like the funeral procession for the man called Batti, where only the cat knew how to express what everyone was feeling?

I am still busy with the names of flowers and I have just learnt to recognise the Spectacular Primrose and here it is, a great bank of absurdly bright pinkness. A Fritillary butterfly, its dark orange wings flecked with little black hieroglyphs, settles on one of the flowers and is poised there, shivering with life.

After an hour and a half we are on the crest of the mountains which marks the modern dividing line between France and Italy. From this high point we have access to all sides of our own valley. If we set off in a westerly direction we would eventually see the broken roofs of the village where the houses are trapped like flies in a spider's web of brambles and briar rose and the thick tendrils of Russian vine. And I suppose we could find our bottles of water still leaning disconsolately against the shrine for the mother of the four blind children.

Going east we could take the unpaved military road that was built after the First World War. Then we could follow a succession of paths that would bring us into the magical amphitheatre dip in the land where there is a flat table of stone that was used for sacrifices long ago. From there it's an easy descent to the scattering of dwellings known as the Plain of the Dove and we could even go to the terrace where we put up our tent for the night and look for the lost pair of sunglasses in their case that should be hiding somewhere among the grasses and the flowers.

Continuing along the rim of the crest we would cross the Pass of the Bowl and then we could try one more time to reach Tuvo from above, struggling through the raspberry bushes and the nut bushes, until we were again confronted by that wooden gate standing all on its own beside a lolling black water pipe. We could phone Armando on his mobile and maybe now he would remember more about what to do next.

If we kept to the high ground, the mountains stretching out on all sides of us like the waves of a vast sea, we could take the path that looks as though it has been drawn with a finger along the steep flank of the land. That would take us to the little hut of Carmo, the grass we cut for our bed still smelling sweet and tinged with an edge of green.

Then home again, going the way that Old Tunin and La Muta and all their family used to go, until we recognised the outline of Adriana's house with the stones on the verandah, the sullen cats, the chickens in their shed, the rabbits muffled in the dark of a cellar. Then it would just be a matter of following the paved road to the lower village where the light of the shop is sure to be burning.

Nanda would see at once that we were too tired to walk any further, so she would ask the butcher if he could take us back to our house in his white van. And if the butcher was already in his pyjamas, she could ask Nella the post office lady who has since retired from her job, but is still always willing to do anything to help, no matter how late or inconvenient.

Nella driving us home in her car, as she did before in April 1999, when I was first here. We reach the post box by the entrance to our track, but Nella says she will take us all the way, so we do the last bumpy stage of the journey and maybe a fox or a tabby cat or a wild pig is briefly frozen in the headlights.

'Mind the toad!' I say to Nella, but she has already seen it. She stops and waits and the toad also stops and waits, facing the danger. I get out of the car and pick it up to move it to one side, feeling the bones inside its soft-skinned body pushing against my hands.

And here is the little parking space with a new metal railing as a protection against the steep drop down to the terraces below. The olive tree that was broken when Herman's tumbling car crashed against it is covered with a display of young branches and the hard green fruits of this year's harvest are already taking shape.

We climb out of Nella's car and thank her for her kindness and she says, it's nothing, and looks at us with her big tired eyes. I hear the water dripping into the tank where a few tadpoles are still busy with the strange task of metamorphosis from one sort of a creature into another. I remember that

I must cut back the ivy, which is again beginning to spread its tendrils across the broken fragment of the tombstone I found on the ground outside the cemetery in the upper village, where I suppose he and I might lie one day, side by side under the earth.

---

But all that is conjecture and for the moment we are still on the old funeral path that leads out of the valley. It takes us across the border and down to the village on the other side. We spend the night in a hotel and the next morning we return, back the way we have come. It's odd how the eye notices the same things it noticed before and the same brief and floating thoughts pass through the mind. A clump of marjoram. The peel from an apple. The flowers on which the butterfly was poised. The traces of our passing hanging in the air like the scent of fox or strawberry. I imagine a solemn line of men and women walking home, freed from the weight of the coffin they were carrying. They are busy watching the path while following the pattering movement of their own thoughts.

The sky has been growing dark. There is a clap of thunder, which ricochets around the bowl of the mountains and it begins to rain in big heavy drops. We take shelter alongside the upturned roots of a fallen tree. We have two umbrellas, but the rain beats at us from all sides and I feel it running in a cold trickle down my neck. When the rain has become less intense, we set off again, going back by the same way that we have come.

# A Little Party

25 July 2010

I want to see everyone I have been talking to gathered together on our terrace. I will give them food and wine and maybe I will even make a photograph of them all looking out across the valley, although when it comes to it I only take a couple of pictures of people sitting round the table and I don't get the light right, so their faces are partially obscured in shadow.

It has to be a lunch because Ida goes to bed so early in the evening. After a bit of asking around, we decide on a date. Herman makes nine invitation cards with a drawing of an old man who looks a bit like Giovanin, sitting by a fire and talking to someone who could be me, listening to him with her head bowed in concentration. Inside there is a list of the names of all the invitees, so people know whom to expect: Adriana; Armando and Ida; Eliana and her husband Massimo (although I know he can't come because he is giving a piano recital on that day) and their little baby Emanuele; Nanda and Agostina and her husband Mario; Tunin and Terzina and Nella and Armando's daughter Rosanna and her husband Sergio who is Old Tunin's grandson, along with their two sons if they are free and would like to join us. I wonder about inviting Giovanin, in spite of the fact that there is no chance of him coming, but even the idea feels like an imposition, so I leave him out.

I go to see Agostina and she is delighted with the picture on the card. She opens it and reads out the names and shakes her head and bites her lip and says what a wonderful thing to do, but she can't leave her husband Mario on his own any more, not since he had the last stroke, which kept him in hospital for more than two weeks. And he can't come because he is nervous in company. She tells me that while he was in hospital a sort of miracle took place: their dead son appeared to him as real as life and he spoke in a clear voice and told his father not to worry, he was there, waiting for the time when they could all be together again.

At this point Mario walks into the kitchen and it's true that he looks much happier than I have ever seen him. There is a new lightness in his expression. Agostina shows him the invitation and he smiles and takes my hand to thank me, and before I leave he presents me with a huge red onion wrapped up in newspaper and Agostina gives me some green beans in a paper bag.

Nanda is also delighted with the invitation and she lets the man who has come with a delivery of yoghurt and butter and other things for the refrigerated display compartment have a look at it and he likes it too. She puts the card up in the place where she used to have copies of the priest's diary. She says she can't come because she can't leave the shop, but she knows I understand and of course I do.

I post an invitation to Tunin and Terzina and a few days later she phones to say that Tunin's head is spinning and he has told her that he doesn't want to go to a party; if he goes anywhere it will be on his own with a dog to his mushroom patch in the mountains and when he gets there he hopes to spend the night sleeping out under the full moon. Terzina says she plans to abandon him to his madness and to come on her own by bus as far as the lower village and then she can do the last bit of the journey with Adriana.

On the morning of the party, Nella says she has such a bad migraine headache that she's terribly sorry but she can't go anywhere and then Eliana tells me that Tunin has chosen this day of all days to drive off to his mushrooms and now Terzina is so angry and upset she can only stay at home and weep. 'He is eighty-seven and she is eighty-four, but they still quarrel like teenagers,' says Eliana.

---

Armando and Ida are the first guests to arrive. She approaches the house with the enthusiasm of a young girl out visiting. She is wearing a white blouse with little flowers embroidered on it and she is carrying a dish of *torta verde* wrapped in a cloth.

I can see Armando standing and staring towards Tuvo, which is now entirely hidden by the leaves on the summer trees. When I come to greet him he says he wants to see the tadpoles in the water tank, so I take him there and he swishes his hand rather impatiently through the spirals of green weed. He admires the maidenhair ferns, which he tells me make a good drink, boiled in water, when you are having trouble with peeing. Then he realises he has forgotten to bring his wine. He has left his car parked halfway along the track, so he sets off in the hot sunshine, his left leg swinging out very stiffly because of the artificial hip joint and something that is wrong with his knee.

Adriana arrives with her daughter Eliana. The baby, who has just had his first birthday, is sitting bolt upright in a pushchair, sparkling with the same intense energy that characterises his mother. Adriana has also brought her own wine along with six eggs from her chickens wrapped in newspaper. She holds my hand and stares quietly into my face before offering a soft cheek to be kissed.

We enter the house where the food is laid out on the table: more *torta verde*, salted olives from our trees and cheese and salami from Nanda. I have printed out some black-and-white photographs on A4 sheets of paper and fixed them with clothes pegs to a string stretched across the wall. Adriana looks at the picture of the Hermit's beehive perched on the edge of a high cliff and wishes she had gone there with Arturo when he had offered to take her. She looks at the picture of the stone wall of Carmo with her husband's name carved into it and the date, 18 August 1944. 'I was still a girl then,' she says.

Armando appears with his wine. He wants to know why we have that little statue of Saint Francis along the track. I tell him it's to make the hunters pause for a moment before they shoot the songbirds and he nods his head wisely as if he has heard about such hunters but has never come across one himself; then he changes the subject and asks how many pages I have now written and he sucks in his breath when I tell him.

Rosanna, his pretty daughter, arrives, along with her husband who is Old Tunin's grandson. Their son is with them as well, looking just like that photograph of Old Tunin when he stands beside the *padrone*, but the stifled rage has gone with the passing of the generations. More bottles of wine and Rosanna has brought a dish of stuffed zucchini flowers.

We all go on to the terrace where there are chairs and a round table set out under the shade of the wisteria's clambering tendrils, which would envelop the whole house and most of this part of the garden if we gave it half a chance. Before we begin to eat, Herman pours out glasses of prosecco and I give a little speech. I say that I hope everyone will like the book if it is eventually translated into Italian and that being here in the valley has made me think that time past and time present and time future is like a vast landscape and we are walking through it on a tracery of thin paths. To my surprise everyone says, yes, it's true, and they burst out clapping.

Then we eat. Nine of us sitting together, while the shifting clouds of an

imminent thunderstorm draw close. The old people again start talking about the war and Adriana says that for a long time after it had ended her dreams were filled with the sound of machine-gun fire. Armando is describing how to throw a hand grenade, the one with a long wooden handle, and Ida says she wishes Pino were here because he had so many stories to tell and with that everyone pauses to think about him.

Later, when we have eaten the *torta verde* and a rabbit stew, which I tried to cook in a traditional manner, and *pannacotta* and pancakes filled with cherries from Ida's tree, Armando suddenly announces that he wants to take me and my husband to find Giovanin in the high mountain place where he spends several weeks during the summer, sleeping in the open under a piece of canvas. He says the place is somewhere not far from the Pass of the Garlands and we can get our car quite close, and he thinks he can manage the last bit of the walk.

'Giovanin only has this much water,' says Armando, pinching the little finger of his left hand with the thumb and first finger of his right hand. 'Call me on my mobile next week and we'll decide when to go and see him.'

The soft babble of talk goes on until the church bell from the lower village strikes four times and after a pause the church bell in the upper village agrees with this calculation. Everyone gets ready to leave. Ida folds the cloth that held the *torta verde* and puts it into a plastic bag. Armando says he would like the empty bottles back, once we have finished all the wine.

The wind has picked up and dark clouds are moving in across the tops of the mountains. When we walk through the room with the photographs, they are flapping on the wall like little flags, tugging at the pegs that hold them in place.

We go out into the parking space and we all stop to look at the green olives on a tree, trying to work out if this promises to be a good harvest.

Adriana climbs into her daughter's car and gazes at us wistfully through the window, moving the fingers of her right hand towards the palm in a gesture of farewell. They are the first to leave. The others follow. We watch them go.

# ACKNOWLEDGEMENTS

My husband Herman has been my first reader.

Our friends in the village and in the valley made this book possible and I hope I have done credit to their trust and their generosity. Any mistakes or omissions are entirely my responsibility.

*Thin Paths* began as a series of five stories written for BBC Radio: 'An Italian Bestiary'. I would like to thank Mary Ward-Lowery, radio producer, friend and wonderful enthusiast.

Dan Franklin, Gill Coleridge and Tom Avery have nurtured this project from its tentative early beginnings.

www.vintage-books.co.uk